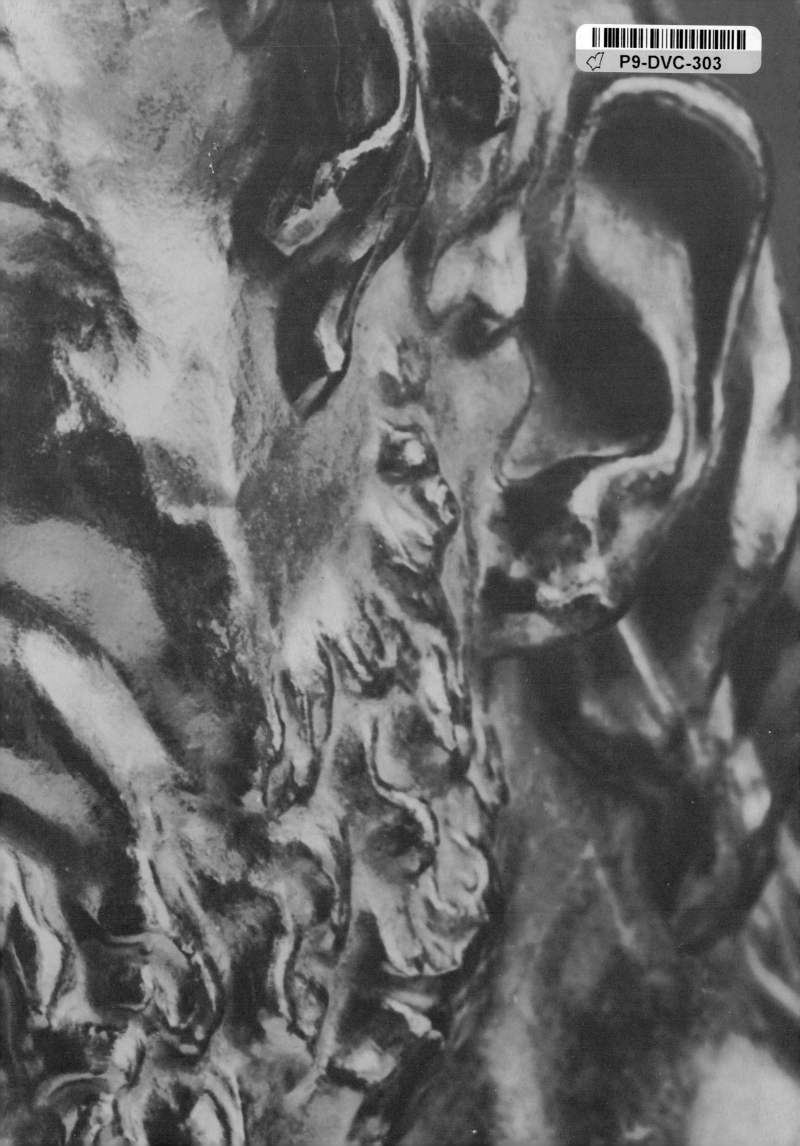

The World of
Rodin

LIFE WORLD LIBRARY

LIFE NATURE LIBRARY

TIME READING PROGRAM

THE LIFE HISTORY OF THE UNITED STATES

LIFE SCIENCE LIBRARY

INTERNATIONAL BOOK SOCIETY

GREAT AGES OF MAN

TIME-LIFE LIBRARY OF ART

TIME-LIFE LIBRARY OF AMERICA

FOODS OF THE WORLD

THIS FABULOUS CENTURY

The World of Rodin

1840-1917

by William Harlan Hale
and
the Editors of TIME-LIFE BOOKS

with Photographs by Lee Boltin and Dmitri Kessel

TIME-LIFE BOOKS, New York

About the Author

William Harlan Hale is a journalist, historian and novelist. A graduate of Yale University, he published his first book, a study of cultural change in 19th Century Europe, when he was 21. Since then he has worked as an editor and writer for a number of national magazines, including *Horizon*, FORTUNE, *The New Republic*, and *The Reporter*, and he has published several other books, principally on American historical subjects. As Chief of the Office of Public Affairs of the United States High Commission in Austria in the early 1950s, Mr. Hale was responsible for introducing many aspects of American cultural life to postwar European audiences and, in turn, acquired an intimate and varied knowledge of art and architecture abroad. He is now a freelance writer and editor.

The Consulting Editor

H. W. Janson is Professor of Fine Arts at New York University, where he is also Chairman of the Department of Fine Arts at Washington Square College. Among his many publications are *History of Art* and *The Sculpture of Donatello*.

The Consultant for This Book

Ruth Mirolli is Assistant Professor in the Department of Art at the University of Maryland. Dr. Mirolli has lectured and taught at Boston University, the National Gallery of Fine Arts in Washington and New York University, where she earned her doctorate. She is presently working on a book, *Introduction to Sculpture*, to be published by the New York Graphic Society.

On the Slipcase

Silhouetted against the evening sky, Rodin's *The Thinker* broods over the artist's grave at Meudon, the Paris suburb where he spent many of his last years.

End Papers

Front: Furrowed with age and the marks of a lifetime of hard work, the face of an old man named Bibi, a Parisian handyman, served Rodin for a powerful early character portrayal, *The Man with the Broken Nose. Back:* Rodin's *Sorrow*—eyes shut tight, lips parted in a sign of anguish—is less a study of an individual than of a state of emotion.

TIME-LIFE BOOKS

EDITOR: Maitland A. Edey
Executive Editor: Jerry Korn
Text Director: Martin Mann
Art Director: Sheldon Cotler
Chief of Research: Beatrice T. Dobie
Picture Editor: Robert G. Mason
Assistant Text Directors: Ogden Tanner, Diana Hirsh
Assistant Art Director: Arnold C. Holeywell
Assistant Chief of Research: Martha T. Goolrick

PUBLISHER: Walter C. Rohrer
Assistant Publisher: Carter Smith
General Manager: John D. McSweeney
Business Manager: John Steven Maxwell
Production Manager: Louis Bronzo

Sales Director: Joan D. Manley
Promotion Director: Beatrice K. Tolleris
Managing Director, International: John A. Millington

TIME-LIFE LIBRARY OF ART

SERIES EDITOR: Robert Morton
Associate Editor: Diana Hirsh
Editorial staff for *The World of Rodin:*
Text Editor: Jay Brennan
Picture Editor: Jane Scholl
Designer: Paul Jensen
Staff Writers: John von Hartz, Kelly Tasker
Chief Researcher: Martha T. Goolrick
Researchers: Evelyn Constable, Catherine Ireys, Susan Jonas, Lynda Kefauver, Patricia Maye, Suzanne Seixas
Assistant to the Designer: Mervyn Clay

EDITORIAL PRODUCTION
Color Director: Robert L. Young
Assistant: James J. Cox
Copy Staff: Rosalind Stubenberg, Patricia Miller, Florence Keith
Picture Department: Dolores A. Littles, Beth Dagenhardt
Traffic: Arthur A. Goldberger

The following individuals and departments of Time Inc. helped to produce this book: LIFE staff photographers Carlo Bavagnoli and Dmitri Kessel; Editorial Production, Robert W. Boyd Jr.; Editorial Reference, Peter Draz; Picture Collection, Doris O'Neil; Photographic Laboratory, George Karas; TIME-LIFE News Service, Murray J. Gart; Correspondent Maria Vincenza Aloisi (Paris).

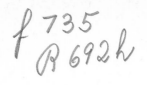
Contents

STEICHEN
MDCCCII

I

Disturber
of the Peace

Paris in the spring of 1889 was a city of sensations. In April it narrowly escaped a coup d'état when General Georges Boulanger, the "man on horseback" who had threatened to overthrow the Third Republic with the aid of royalist cohorts, suddenly decamped to Belgium to join his mistress. Five weeks later booming guns proclaimed the centennial of the great revolution of 1789 and the opening of a Universal Exposition to mark the anniversary. The fairgrounds on the Champ-de-Mars were the scene of a shimmer and pride of exhibits. One could marvel at technological wonders in the block-long Galerie des Machines, ascend the vertiginous new tower designed by Alexandre Gustave Eiffel, ogle exotic dancers in the "Street of Cairo," or inspect pavilions displaying the riches of France's African and Asian colonies and the latest art of Paris itself.

Of all these glories the prize exhibit, beflagged and illuminated, was the 984-foot tower, the tallest creation yet made by man. From distant America, Thomas A. Edison joined its admirers by publicly thanking God for "so great a structure," but there were those who deplored it as a monstrosity, and a dangerous one at that. Intellectuals were repelled by it, and property owners around the Champ-de-Mars had brought suit to stop its construction, fearing it might topple on them.

Below the tower, in the Exposition's sculpture hall, stood an exhibit that in its way was sensational and controversial too. It was a life-sized plaster figure of an aging man in a ragged shroud, his body gnarled and bent forward in suffering, his face pitted and creased, his hands exaggeratedly large. The whole work, with its rough surfaces, ridges, lumps and welts, looked raw, unbalanced, incomplete, incoherent. Many observers found it totally baffling. Traditionally, a piece of sculpture was supposed to present not only a recognizable theme—patriotic, allegorical, lyrical, or all three—but correct proportions, poise and polish.

The statue indeed was based on a patriotic theme, as its label—"Figure of a man for the sculpture group, *Burghers of Calais*"—suggested. The title referred to an incident during the Hundred Years' War when six leading citizens of beleaguered Calais offered their lives to their English conquerors in hopes of preventing the devastation of their city. But the sculpted burgher was not shown in a classic, noble pose; rather, he looked anguished. Moreover, the sculptor seemed simply to have thrown heaps and blobs of clay on the figure without taking the trouble to refine or finish it.

To Parisians who knew their way around the city's art scene, the innovations were not altogether surprising. The burgher's creator was Auguste Rodin, and at 48 he was making a name as an artist of uncomfortable boldness and originality. Only a few months earlier a fashionable gallery had plucked him from relative obscurity and put on a show of 36 of his sculptures, jointly with 70 paintings by the Impressionist Claude Monet, as the work of two artists most identified with "new currents." No less esteemed a critic than Octave Mirbeau had pronounced the show a colossal success, and lauded its two "wonderful" artists. "It is they," he wrote in *Echo de Paris*, "who in our century are the most glorious, the most complete embodiment of the two arts, painting and sculpture." After such an accolade it was easy for Rodin to obtain a prominent exhibitor's place at the Exposition, and inevitable for those who had previously dismissed his work as harsh and awkward to take a second, closer look. Even if their verdict remained the same, one conclusion was unarguable: whatever Rodin put his hand to exuded an overwhelming power, a force untamed.

What was equally intriguing, to those who came to know him personally at this major turning point in his career, was that Rodin himself reflected these qualities. Although he was only five feet four inches tall, he gave the impression of a man cast in a giant's mold. His body was muscular, with massive shoulders and broad hands. A high, heavy brow and a full red beard made his head seem unusually large. He had a prominent nose and penetrating blue eyes, often half shut or gazing in apparent abstraction. A distinct animal magnetism, an aura of collected passion, conveyed itself to many men and still more women. One male visitor to his studio thought that "he seems to descend from the clouds . . . from an assembly of the immortals." The somewhat snobbish novelist and critic Edmond de Goncourt disdained his "common features" but went on to concede that Rodin struck him as "a man such as I imagine Christ's disciples looked like."

Both in his person and in his work Rodin shocked yet attracted. He could not be overlooked—eventually, not even escaped. But the times in which he lived, after decades dominated by solid bourgeois standards, were receptive to the unconventional and the daring. At the new Moulin Rouge, Yvette Guilbert was singing her bawdy songs with an innocent air, and cancan dancers were packing in the top-hatted *boulevardiers;* the painter Toulouse-Lautrec immortalized that scene. At Maxim's, bejeweled beauties aptly known as *les grandes horizontales* impartially graced the arm of *nouveau riche* or Russian grand duke. On a more erudite level, the new and the original were also winning plaudits. In the sophisticated drawing rooms of the Faubourg Saint-Germain the hardbitten realism of Émile Zola's writings was much admired, and so was Anatole France's urbane novel of pagan Alexandria, *Thaïs.* The golden

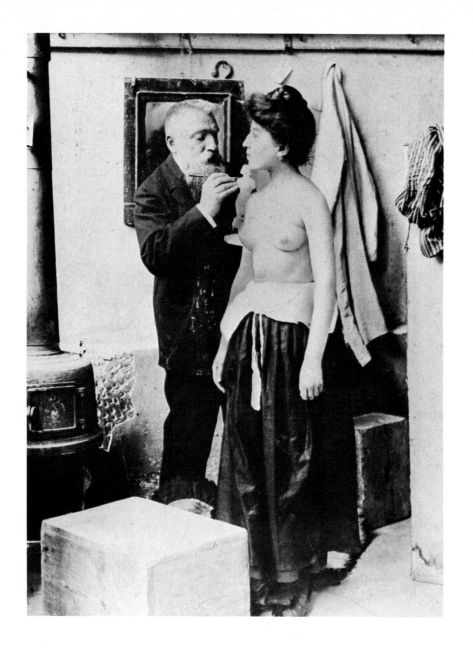

Rodin's technique of modeling in clay involved a painstaking study of the outlines of the body. First he scrutinized his subject from different angles before deciding on the profiles he wanted to capture. Then, working as shown here, very close to the model, he successively reproduced each profile, turning his stand and the model until he had completely circled the body. Unlike most sculptors of his day, he usually relied on his eye rather than on calipers to check the accuracy of the clay outlines against the original. "The model," he said, "teaches us what we should do," but he warned students that this deceptively simple approach required keen powers of observation and exceptional hand-eye coordination.

age, *la belle époque*, of Paris was at hand, and as if to mark its onset an unfamiliar young man began to be welcomed at fashionable salons: one Marcel Proust, not yet 20, a somewhat effete, precocious dandy who would in time become the era's sovereign analyst.

Rodin, too, was seen in the salons; his strange sculptural notions, his arresting person, made invitations inevitable. But he was a presence somewhat apart, a man who fascinated yet enraged people. He was a genius who gave fresh impetus to sculpture, the greatest master of the art since Michelangelo and Bernini, a virtuoso raging to bring life out of clay. At the same time he had a countryman's earthiness and pigheadedness and insensitivity. He could be distinctly boorish, even brutal. Although he and Monet were born within two days of one another, befriended each other, exhibited together, and Rodin often visited Monet's country retreat in Giverney, he once burst out: "I don't give a damn for Monet, I don't care a damn for anybody. I am interested only in myself." Both detractors and admirers saw the conflicting strains within Rodin; there is scarcely a contemporary comment about him, favorable or unfavorable, that does not contain a built-in "on the other hand": "He is a monster, but he is also . . ." "He is a remarkable sculptor, but he is also . . ."

On some points, all observers agreed. He was a man of extraordinary vitality, constantly absorbed with the human body—especially woman's. A typical scene in his studio was a lavish nudist spectacle. Unlike other sculptors who employed one model to mount a stand and assume a fixed pose, Rodin liked to have a bevy of nudes freely walking about the place or reclining, while he dashed off sketches of one or another as a fleeting gesture caught his interest. One frequent visitor wrote: "He silently savors the beauty of the life which plays through them, he admires the suppleness of this young woman who bends to pick up a chisel, the delicate grace of this other who raises her arms to gather her golden hair above her head, the nervous vigor of a man who walks across the room; and when this one or that makes a movement that pleases him, he instantly asks that the pose be kept. Quick, he seizes the clay, and a little figure is under way." Rodin worked close—very close—to his female models. One day a studio assistant saw him lean over a model who had particularly pleased him and kiss her tenderly—on the belly. According to the assistant, this was "an adoring tribute to Nature for the countless favors he had received from her" (meaning Nature).

The abundance of active, naked models served a purpose. Not since the athletic contests of Greek and Roman times had sculptors had the opportunity to observe unclothed human bodies in constant motion—and Rodin was above all interested in conveying motion. Yet some men saw him not as a sculptor recapturing the drama of the body in action but as a rampant goat. One was the poet Paul Claudel, who had personal reason to dislike Rodin. (The man had, Claudel claimed with considerable justice, ruined the life of his sister Camille.) Claudel wrote that Rodin had "the big, bulging eyes of a lecher. When he worked he had his nose right on the model and the clay. Did I say his nose? A boar's snout, rather, behind which lurked a pair of icy blue pupils."

There was never any doubt of the eroticism in Rodin's sculpture. Some of it was mild, and in acceptable French tradition. Rodin's *The Kiss*, with its naked, embracing lovers, was no franker than the amorous couples portrayed by such 18th Century rococo painters as François Boucher and Jean-Honoré Fragonard, and was in fact bought in 1888 by the French government. *The Kiss*, however, was bland in comparison to other Rodin portrayals of amorous activity—not bought by the government in Rodin's lifetime—like *Idyll* and *Eternal Springtime (page 110)*, in which the sexual act seems near at hand, and *Thè Ascendancy*, in which the act is in process.

Lecher, demigod, evil eye, prophet, magician in clay or bronze—all these Rodin was or became in people's minds. Obviously a hot-blooded man, all intensity. One who saw that intensity at first hand was the young American devotee of new forms in the dance, Isadora Duncan, who made her way to Rodin's studio to salute the master of new forms in sculpture. The meeting took place in 1900, when Rodin had reached 60, but he was as energetic and compelling as ever. Isadora described the encounter in her own candid way: "He showed his works with the simplicity of the very great. Sometimes he murmured the names for his statues. . . . He ran his hands over them and caressed them. . . . Finally he took a small quantity of clay and pressed it between his palms. He breathed hard as he did so. The heat streamed from him like a radiant furnace. In a few moments he had formed a woman's breast, that palpitated beneath his fingers."

Then they took a cab and went to her studio, where she changed into her tunic and danced for him, stopping to "explain to him my theories for a new dance," only to realize that Rodin was not listening. "He gazed at me with lowered lids, his eyes blazing, and then, with the same expression that he had before his works, he came toward me. He ran his hands over my neck, breast, stroked my arms and ran his hands over my hips, my bare legs and feet. He began to knead my whole body as if it were clay, while from him emanated heat that scorched and melted me. My whole desire was to yield to him my entire being, and, indeed, I would have done so if it had not been that my absurd upbringing caused me to become frightened and I withdrew and sent him away bewildered. . . . What a pity! How often I have regretted this childish miscomprehension which lost to me the divine chance of giving my virginity to the Great God Pan himself, to the Mighty Rodin. Surely Art and all Life would have been richer thereby!"

When Rodin met Isadora Duncan she was a shy young American-born dancer who had come to Paris seeking acceptance of her new ideas about dance and theater. Frequenting the Louvre's classical galleries as Rodin had done 40 years before, she plunged into a study of ancient Greece that deeply influenced both her art and her life. She danced in Grecian tunics (above) and often wore such garb off stage, as in the gently reflective camera portrait below.

The fire and impetuosity that Isadora saw were basic to Rodin's makeup. He was capable of instantaneous response to sight or shape—or to impulse. This, over and beyond his sheer masculine drive, was the clue to much of his art. Rodin sought to communicate the sense of excitement of the moving human body simply in its flexions and quick changes. To achieve spontaneity, he worked at phenomenal speed, modeling with clay or drawing in pencil in a copybook in rapid response to his model's changing movements, discarding and trying again. In the cellar of the Rodin Museum in Meudon, outside Paris, there are cabinets filled with hundreds of his brief experiments with heads, torsos, legs, arms and hands. He sometimes worked on half a dozen or more heads or hands in a day, molding the clay with his fingers or a penknife—only to dismiss all the results.

In such urgency and hunger for creation, his natural medium was the malleable clay. He made innumerable small clay models—maquettes —until he had a design to his liking. Then he had an assistant build —from wood, wire, pipes and nails—an armature, or skeleton, approximately one third to one half the size of the figure he planned ultimately to produce. Using a plaster cast of his original maquette as a guide, Rodin next built up a clay replica on the armature, heaping it with the blobs and pellets that were a hallmark of his work, altering the design as it took shape under his hands. When satisfied with this larger model, which was kept moist with wet cloths so that he could continually rework the clay, he set his assistants to building a full-scale armature. Then Rodin began the process again—the laying on of the clay, giving a bold jab here to bring out a grimace of the flex of a biceps, using the slightest touch of a finger there to form a quiver of movement or play of light.

Next, a plaster cast was made of the completed figure, perhaps to serve as the base for a bronze cast. Or, on occasion, the clay figure was fired in a kiln to produce a terra-cotta version. If one of his works was to be reproduced in marble Rodin seldom bothered with the task; this process he left almost entirely to studio technicians. Using a plaster cast of the work as a model, they would bore holes to predetermined depths into a stone block and then cut away until they had duplicated the original cast. It was only rarely that Rodin applied a correcting chisel; he found working with stone dull, and much preferred the challenge of clay. Molding it, pummeling it, he demonstrated his belief that broken surfaces were the essence of sculpture. The bolder elements of a work, he believed, should stand forth to catch the light; weaker elements should be hollowed to hold the shade; highlights and hollows should complement one another to express meaning. "To model shadow is to bring out the thought," he once remarked. Without his guiding hand, marble reproductions of his work often came out smoother and more polished than the originals.

Rodin's preference for working in a soft material was by no means unusual. The method was well within the tradition of Western sculpture, and few artists since Michelangelo had tried to emulate the Florentine master's method of wrestling with stone, "liberating the figure from the marble that imprisons it," as he himself put it. Nor was Rodin unique in his dramatic expression; in this he had learned much from the sculpture of the baroque era. What was extraordinary about him was his virtuosity with his chosen medium, the pungency of his attack, his ability to give tangible form to emotion. No matter if a raised hand or moving leg or turned neck did not conform to correct, academic proportion: did the sculpture speak?

Rodin was not only one of the most expressive of sculptors, but one of the most prolific. He turned out thousands of busts, single figures, groups and fragments. The very profusion of his work has done him a kind of injustice: because history knows him as a sculptor, many of his other talents have been overlooked. He was a tireless draftsman and watercolorist; some 7,000 of his drawings, preserved in the recesses of the Rodin Museum in Paris, have never even been exhibited. He was also, especially in his thirties, a painter in oils. Moreover, before he began to earn a steady living from sculpture, he was one of the most skilled professional designers and decorators in France, turning out everything from carved bedsteads for the boudoirs of fashionable courtesans to portico caryatids to designs for Sèvres porcelain. An interest in the medieval led him to become an architectural historian, author of *The Cathedrals of France*, which he illustrated with structural drawings. He was a leading collector of classical art, a private and public orator on esthetics, a serious student of letters—all these and amorist too.

He began his years as a decorator's apprentice in a run-down working-class quarter of Paris and rounded them out as one of the most prestigious and sought-after personalities in Europe. The road between was long and hard. Until he was in his forties sculpting for his own satisfaction was a luxury; economic need forced him to spend most of his time in everyday work for pay, first as an artisan, then as a decorator with orders of his own. With the 1880s he began to receive some recognition—a Salon prize here, an interested buyer there—for the sculptures closest to his heart. But it was only in 1889, with his show with Monet and his sensation soon thereafter at the centennial Exposition, that Rodin was established as a major influence radiating from the art capital of the world.

Rodin liked to describe himself as a man of the people, recalling that "until the age of 50 I had all the worries of poverty." Life thereafter was very different. Pursued by patrons and titled ladies, his studio crowded with young followers and famous sitters, he was hailed as the greatest sculptor of the time. In his final years the *maître* graciously received a visit from Edward VII of England but coolly turned down an application by Kaiser Wilhelm II for a bust of his imperial self. George Bernard Shaw paid a handsome £1,000—the equivalent of at least $18,000 today—for a portrait bust in marble. The actress Eleanora Duse came to recite for Rodin and Wanda Landowska to play her harpsichord for him, as Isadora had danced for him. The painter Paul Cézanne, grateful for his handshake, dropped to his knees before him. He was awarded a doctorate from Oxford and the gold emblem of a Grand Officer of the Legion of Honor.

Poets as well as statesmen celebrated him. The German poet Rainer Maria Rilke, who briefly became his secretary, rhapsodized that Rodin's figures were "invincible . . . transcendent . . . unsurpassable realizations." Guillaume Apollinaire, one of the hard-living *bande Picasso* that gathered in Montmartre cafés around a young firebrand painter from Catalonia, hailed Rodin's work as "sublime." Rodin's worldwide impact was unequaled by any artist until Picasso himself moved into his prime. Between the two men, who probably never met, there were striking similarities in invention, personal magnetism and power, though a later generation might regard them as worlds apart.

Continuing controversy was also a part of Rodin's fame. There was a near-riot in the city of Nancy in 1892 when a crowd broke up the unveiling of a monument by Rodin to protest the sketchy way in which he had sculpted the horses. There was persistent furor throughout the 1890s over a statue he was making of the late novelist Honoré de Balzac; eventually the completed work was rejected as "artistically insufficient" by the literary society that had commissioned it. ("An ignoble and insane nightmare," one critic called it.) And—the ultimate scandal—at the Chicago World's Fair of 1893, Rodin's *The Kiss* was put away as unfit for public showing.

The Fair had been planned to outdo the recent Paris Exposition and to commemorate the 400th anniversary of America's discovery. A vast "White City" arose beside Lake Michigan, with classical domes, plazas and lagoons vying for attention with a midway, a giant Ferris wheel and another "Street of Cairo." Mrs. Potter Palmer, Chicago's leading hostess and art collector, was one of the Fair's commissioners; the well-known American sculptor Augustus Saint-Gaudens was one of its designers. Saint-Gaudens was so elated as plans for its Palace of Fine

Arts took shape that he exclaimed to his fellow committeemen, "Look here, do you realize that this is the greatest meeting of artists since the Fifteenth Century!"

Rodin was of course among the artists that the Americans wanted to include, but when the crates bringing his contributions were opened, the chief exhibit was found to be *The Kiss*, with its strongly wrought lovers. To the shocked Fair authorities it did no good to point out that *The Kiss* had recently been acquired by the French state itself for 20,000 francs. It simply would not do for public display in Chicago. So, while fairgoers were encouraged to buy tickets to leer at belly dancers on the midway, *The Kiss* was relegated to an inner chamber at the Fair, admission upon personal application only. Yet prudery did not completely prevail. Not long after *The Kiss* was first shown, or rather not shown, at Chicago, an American collector living in England ordered a copy of it in Pentelic marble for £1,000, specifying through his agent that he wanted it also to be as explicit as possible: *"l'organe génital de l'homme doit être complet."*

Eventually *The Kiss* (not necessarily *complet*) became so widely known as to be almost a stock image on the jackets of romantic novels and books on sexology. Rodin's muscular, brooding *Thinker*, sculpted in 1880, was fated to gain even greater fame and to become almost a talisman—perhaps the most widely reproduced sculpture of all time. There would be mass-produced "Thinker" book ends available at drugstore counters in metal or plastic; "Thinker" lamp bases in brass; limestone "Thinker" replicas for the portals of circulating libraries and college philosophy departments; prints of it in advertisements for physical culture, for self-improvement and even for an electrical appliance with a built-in "brain."

Thus popular tastes caught up with Rodin, while at the same time the educated tastes he had sought to impress began to bypass him. He became overaccepted, overexposed—ironically, chiefly through a few figures that were hardly his best. The highly original *Burghers of Calais* group, and his crowning work, the statue of Balzac, on which he labored for seven years, never became favorites. Serious viewers wearied of much of his art and many came to regard it as dated and banal, especially as the preferences of a new time moved into directions other than his.

Seen against the background of his time, Rodin stands forth as somewhat larger than life—as one of that breed of stormy titans who held an era transfixed by the power of their imagination and the huge scope of their labors. One thinks of Balzac of the vast *Comédie Humaine*, of Victor Hugo of *Les Misérables*, of Tolstoi of *War and Peace*, peopling whole worlds of their own; and of Zola, with his cycle of novels about one passion-driven French family, and of Richard Wagner, creating his tempestuous *Der Ring des Nibelungen*.

Like them, Rodin is also a man of the great theme, a personification of every sort of passion, an artist expressing all the joys and tragedies of existence. His own sculpture court is a whole population—rising youths, happy or sad lovers, delightsome mistresses, sage citizens, seers,

Rodin's *The Kiss (above)* has always entranced the public, even when his work was out of vogue among artists. Originally a half-life-sized study for *The Gates of Hell*, it has since been enlarged to more than life size and copied repeatedly in marble. The carefully observed details give the piece its lasting appeal: the tension in the man's right foot and in the hand that touches the woman's thigh contrasts with her yielding pose and suggests that her ardor has almost caught him unaware.

sufferers, worn old men and women, and a fleeting accompaniment of nymphs, sirens, bacchantes, centaurs acting out their classic roles. The realistic mingles with the symbolic in allegories of the awakening and corruption of flesh, of harsh seasons and the rebirth of spring. Rodin has the grand manner that one associates above all with Michelangelo, in which all bodies are surrounded with the aura of some fateful meaning, and in which even the small are made to seem mighty. Everything in Rodin is large or appears to be; he is perhaps the last sculptor in history whose works are described as "statues"; since Rodin, one speaks of "figures." His sense for the monumental was such that he planned as his ultimate achievement a portal of Renaissance proportions to be known as *The Gates of Hell,* based on themes from Dante's *Inferno*—a project never brought to completion, although Rodin spent much of his time for almost 40 years peopling it with nearly 200 figures, including the original of *The Thinker.*

Underneath Rodin's art lay the dedication of a volcanic, driven man, one at odds with the conformities and conventions of the middle-class world around him. To him, an artist worthy of the name had to speak truly of the human condition—sometimes splendid, more often troubled and tragic—and he had to convey his awareness of that condition through every gesture and muscle of his work. Rodin had his religion: it was the human body, which he once described as "a temple that marches . . . a moving architecture." Its every motion, inflection, even passing hint of expression, were embodiments of man's estate, crying out to be seen and fully felt. Moreover—and here is the heart of Rodin's feeling and thinking—every form itself was a symbol, a paradigm, a shadow of what lay within. "Lines and colors are only . . . the symbols of hidden realities," he said. "Our eyes plunge beneath the surface to the meaning of things, and when afterward we reproduce the form, we endow it with the spiritual meaning which it covers."

This idea, of course, was by no means original with Rodin. The thought that visible things led to a revelation of the invisible had come down all the way from Plato. As Rodin saw it, a mere fragment—an arm, a leg, or a torso sculpted without either arms or legs, or even without a head—might serve to reveal a whole range of yearning or anguish or fulfillment. And all that was true in nature was beautiful in art also: "There is nothing ugly in art, except that which is without character, that is to say, that which offers no outer or inner truth."

Rodin's decision to make sculpture the medium for the expression of these ideas came at a time when the art had fallen in large part into aridity. In his young manhood the sculptor's world was generally confining, distinctly unpromising when compared to the exciting world of painting. While the Impressionists were breaking loose from formula, most sculptors were producing little more than effigies—either a perfectly posed imitation of a classic or a bit of storytelling sentiment. The poet and critic Charles Baudelaire, whom Rodin much admired, regularly inveighed against what seemed to him the preference of most sculptors of the era for drawing-room trivia, their lack both of high seriousness and of invention. Sculpture, once so great, Baudelaire wrote,

Adorned with a starkly lighted black-and-white photograph of *The Kiss,* this French sex manual is only one of countless magazines and books whose covers have exploited the famous statue. Clinical sex studies and romantic novels alike have traded on—and perpetuated—its familiarity. Although he had created an enduring image of sexual love, Rodin in later years dismissed *The Kiss* as "pretty" but conventional, a work in which he had made "no discovery."

had fallen into the hands of "*vaudevillistes*" and copyists who "make free with all periods and all genres." The art had, he charged, lost its relevance to humanity: "No one is cocking his ear to tomorrow's wind, and yet the heroism of modern life surrounds us and presses upon us." These thoughts were close to Rodin's own, though he was rarely as brutal as Baudelaire in voicing them. Once, however, when criticized by the judging committee for his first designs for *The Burghers of Calais*, he retorted, "I am the enemy in Paris of this [prevailing] pompous and Scholastic kind of art. You want me to be a follower of people whose conventional style I despise."

The reasons for the staleness of sculpture, as against the new vivacity of painting, were many. In centuries past, painting and sculpture had stood side by side as partners and equals, thanks to the munificence of the patrons of those times—popes, kings and courtiers. The decline of noble patronage had an especially harmful effect on the sculptor. It was not particularly difficult for a painter to be left to his own resources; all he required, after all, was canvas, paint and brushes—and in due course he made full use of his independence. The sculptor, dependent on costlier materials like bronze and marble, found it far harder to adjust. To be sure, there were new-rich patrons for sculpture, but in general—and this was crucial—they lacked the assurance of their highborn predecessors. Timid in their tastes, they leaned to works that imitated the past or reflected a touch of sentiment, and they favored the artists who would oblige.

Rodin himself blamed the wealthy new middle class of France for much bad art. "Go visit the collectors," he said, "go into their rich bourgeois salons and look around you—you will see only things which are sad, dead, ugly, and without interest." In addition to the private collectors, there was the state, which in France had taken over royalty's role as chief patron. This shift was less than advantageous to artists, considering the hordes of bureaucrats with which they now had to contend. The state's preference in art leaned not only to self-glorification—as had been the case with the Bourbon kings—but to the celebration of civic virtue and sound moral precepts. In 19th Century France these official criteria were pursued with increasing ponderousness and decreasing grace. The state's grand-opera houses, façades, arches and memorials festooned with figures suffocated under their own decorations. A happy combination of sculpture and architecture was rare. Sheer ornament was the rage. As the leading American authority on Rodin, Albert Elsen, has written, when Rodin came on the scene sculpture had become "the stepchild of the arts . . . relegated to decoration."

Moreover, the state's machinery for "administering" art inevitably inhibited men of originality. Beside the Ministry of Fine Arts, which had to approve all designs for public buildings and statuary, stood the veteran Institut de France, in effect the official watchdog of French culture. Among its several branches was the Académie des Beaux-Arts, which in turn ran the celebrated school known as the École des Beaux-Arts —the "Grande École," in the eyes of its students and aspirants. The school was almost the mandatory route to artistic recognition, especially if one won the right to exhibit at the quasi-official annual Salons. Presiding over these "bazaars" (as the painter Jean-Auguste-Dominique Ingres called them) were judges who were themselves almost always school graduates and members of the Academy, and whose rejection of a proffered work could mean financial disaster to an artist. By Rodin's time the Academy-Salon complex had long frozen into a fixed position, and so had most of the sculpture the Academicians produced. By the mid-1860s Zola—a man no less concerned with the state of the arts than Baudelaire—was denouncing the Salon jurors as "timid mediocrities" with "stolen reputations," a "coterie of cooks" who served up only a nondescript "ragout."

Rodin himself, who as a young student could not win admission to the Grande École, was never vindictive to the point of assailing the idea of an official Academy. Indeed, as Albert Elsen has emphasized, Rodin shared many of the Academy's ideas; he staunchly believed in formal discipline and in training young sculptors and painters to produce art that would ennoble and offer tribute to the nation's past. What affronted Rodin, however, was what he saw being produced at the school. It was so committed to convention, he once remarked, that it could never "look truth in the face."

Less than a century earlier the liveliest sculptor in France had been Jean-Antoine Houdon, whose masterwork was a searching likeness of Voltaire in old age *(page 35)*—a psychological tour de force that conveyed all of the man's wit and malice, a portrait so incisive that it stood unchallenged for generations. In later years Houdon went to America to execute two figures of George Washington—one in his Continental Army uniform, handsome and stately, the other in imperial Roman toga, lofty but blank. The latter effort expressed the growing vogue for imitation of the antique that dominated sculpture until well into Rodin's time.

This increasingly modish Neoclassical style above all favored a nostalgia for the distant past. It was a taste for the Neoclassical that caused the Italian Antonio Canova to sculpt Napoleon I, a short, stocky man, as a colossal nude Caesar. The Emperor's earthy sister, Pauline, was similarly cast as an Olympian Venus. The style was professorial, polite. One celebrated practitioner of the Neoclassical was the Danish sculptor Bertel Thorvaldsen. In 1816 Thorvaldsen worked on the restoration of a group of ancient marble statues discovered in the ruins on the Greek island of Aegina, but so doctored them that they emerged as pallid, sexless shapes. Today this would be considered an act of vandalism; at the time, the new look the statues acquired became the rage.

No institution seized on the Neoclassical formula more avidly than did the French Academy. With each decade its teachings increasingly congealed. There was an acceptable *"grande figure"* style, a repertory of correct "classical" gestures to convey such themes as Civic Virtue, Military Courage, Faith, Science, Order, Industry Protecting Labor. There was a prescribed rhetoric of *belles pensées*—uplifting, positive thoughts. The figure itself had always to be bland, immobile, pure. ("But the Greeks," Rodin erupted at one point, "were not like this!")

The noted painter and caricaturist Honoré Daumier was also a talented sculptor. Around 1850 he made this maquette—small clay model—of a shady Parisian type he dubbed *Ratapoil*, a club-wielding ruffian employed by politicians to influence voters. Below is a caricature bust Daumier modeled in the 1830s of an anonymous citizen, now simply known as the *Man with a Flat Head*.

To be sure, below the level of the appointed *grands sujets* were the *petits sujets* that allowed some leeway. There was, inevitably, the Nude, and no opportunity was lost to display it to advantage. Much Salon art, whether sculpture or painting, seemed no more than an invitation to view high-class, cultural bottoms, such as those of the flying nymphs of Adolphe-William Bouguereau's *Les Oréades* or the swelling marble posterior of a kneeling maiden by Lorenzo Bartolini entitled, in heaven's name, *Trust in God*. Rodin would never commit such an indecency.

But for many artists, genteel *pensées* were not enough. For these there was Romanticism, still an artistic force in the mid-19th Century, with its multiple enthusiasms for liberty, for nature, for unleashed emotions, for storm and stress—the boundless, the spontaneous, the savage and exotic. In painting, Romanticism produced its master in Eugène Delacroix, whose themes ranged from revolutionary politics to Arab horsemen in battle with animals. In sculpture, the movement did not fare so well, though Delacroix's heroic painting *Liberty Leading the People* did find its counterpart in François Rude's fiery relief *La Marseillaise (page 53)*, designed for the Arc de Triomphe. It is there today, theatrical but epic and compelling, and one of the very few Romantic masterworks in stone. In large part, sculptors who turned from the bland and would-be classical produced simple anecdotage, preferably with a touch of violence.

Their members included a group that became known as *animaliers*, specialists in producing renditions of large or small beasts that could be shown in savage postures—as human beings, according to the Salon's canons, could not possibly be. The Salon gave space to Antoine-Louis Barye's *Tiger Devouring a Crocodile* and to Emmanuel Frémiet's popular *Gorilla Attacking a Maiden*. Sculptural storytelling ran also to the declamatory and the pathetic: there were innumerable Joans of Arc in all stages of victory and hazard, and the French defeat in the Franco-Prussian War of 1870 led to a memorial *(page 62)* by Antonin Mercié, set up in the frontier town of Belfort, in which "an Alsatian mother seizes the musket falling from the hands of her wounded son and stands on defense against the enemy."

Barye, for one, was a serious and purposeful man; Rodin attended his classes as a young student and admired his studies from nature. But many other popular sculptors of the mid-19th Century wore a withering label, given them by the acidulous Baudelaire: they were *pompiers*, "firemen" without convictions, whose sole aim was to quench the taste of tasteless people with money to burn. One of the most successful *pompiers* of the time was Albert-Ernest Carrier-Belleuse, an engaging, facile, handsome man who ran a virtual factory of sculpture and decoration; with the aid of 20 or more assistants he turned out a huge line of stock studio busts, statuettes, figurines, candelabra and bric-a-brac in popular style. He was a considerable cut above the other *pompiers*, but he too might today be forgotten except that one of his assistants for many years was Auguste Rodin.

There were a few—a very few—superior men who dared strike out on paths of their own. Honoré Daumier, that sardonic critic of human folly and injustice, turned from his prints and paintings to model a small gallery of ruthless images in clay: a blowsy orator, a toothless old wreck of a man, a quixotic, grotesque veteran, *Ratapoil*. This was realism coming forward—with a quality of caricature and social protest. A sculptor whom the young Rodin knew and admired was the inventive Jean-Baptiste Carpeaux, whose dashing style was quite different from Daumier's; he was the favorite sculptor of Napoleon III and his grandiose court, yet a designer of great verve and freshness—as expressed, for instance, in his lively bacchanal, *La Danse*, designed for the front of the Paris Opera.

Still, when an artist of Rodin's cast of mind looked about and considered who had gone long before—a Bernini, a Michelangelo, a Donatello, the sculptors of Greece and the nameless stone carvers of Gothic cathedrals—the sculptural heritage of France seemed sadly depleted. As he saw his opportunity, therefore, it was not to break sharply with tradition—so little of it survived in genuine form in any case —but to seek to revive sculpture and return to its best. In this sense he was one of the most conservative of radicals. As one of his numerous secretaries, Anthony Ludovici, recalled of some observations Rodin once made: "He never claimed that he had introduced anything fresh, but that he had rediscovered what had been long lost by the academicians. The Greeks had possessed it, and so also had the Gothics. But in the official art of the day it was entirely lacking. His contribution . . . was therefore an act of restoration."

This was not the whole truth, by any means. Rodin was retrospective but also adventurous, exploring expressionism and even the abstract. But a time came when he was dismissed as an "eclectic," a collector of old bones of art, when the very premises on which his work was built were challenged and discarded. The great revolution that dawned toward the end of the 19th Century was built on the idea that a work of art need not—indeed, perhaps should not—seek to represent any seen object or event, or induce any "meaning" from it. A work should be an independent creation, subject only to its own laws of form, without reference outside itself.

So Rodin's rhetoric, his emotions, his language of gestures, his symbolism, his affinities with literature, eventually became unfashionable. But during his lifetime he was the embodiment of change. As one artist recalled of his own student days in the late 1870s: "At this time, remember, we were all working at the School, and obliged to follow the old manner of study taught there. But Rodin so vividly impressed us that we took a new start, determined to look out for everything that was good, no matter where it came from or who did it. Seeing Rodin gave us new life."

That life has revived in our time, when the problem of man's estate has again become one of profound concern to the artist. Rodin has his place, then, both as a classic end and as a beginning. As one admirer has remarked, he was to become the Moses of modern sculpture, leading it out of the wilderness, though not himself destined to enter the promised land.

Rodin's Classic Heritage

Although he was often attacked as a revolutionary, Rodin described himself as "a link in the great chain of artists," a man whose art was proudly rooted in the past. His education, in the Paris of the 1850s, was traditional, and he never deliberately rebelled against it. He learned to sculpt at a school that still taught according to 18th Century precepts. After class he haunted the Louvre, where most often he chose to sketch antique Greek sculpture. Working from museum prints of Michelangelo before he could afford a trip to Italy, he began a lifelong study of the master he called "this great benefactor of humanity" and of his predecessor and fellow Florentine, Donatello.

Conscious of his role as an inheritor and transmitter of Western artistic tradition, Rodin, as a Frenchman, was also concerned with his own nation's heritage. Examining French sculpture, he traced an unchanging spirit behind the changing styles of succeeding eras—a spirit that invested the Gothic façades of medieval cathedrals, enlivened the contours of 16th Century nymphs and 17th Century caryatids, and in the 18th Century enhanced rococo mythological groups as well as realistic portrait busts. Rodin's eclectic appreciation contrasted with the academic approach of many of his contemporaries. The quotations that accompany the sculpture on the following pages are from his own writings and conversations, and reflect what he hoped to instill in his countrymen: the confidence to respond directly to art of all ages.

How charming! This young torso, without a head, seems to smile at the light and at the spring, better than eyes and lips could do!

Praxiteles (copy after): *Periboetus*, c. 325 B.C.
MUSÉE DU LOUVRE, PARIS

22

*Greek sculpture is warm, strong, firm, simple,
true to nature, and full of power. It is life
itself . . . the teaching of the academy does not
include a thorough comprehension of either nature
or the Greek.*

Polykleitos (copy after): *Diadoumenos*, c. 430 B.C.

*I know that good low-relief is as full and
as fruitlike as sculpture in the round, that
it is sculpture in the round itself, as in the
friezes of the Parthenon.*

Maidens from Parthenon frieze, 442-438 B.C.

*The impression of mystery is felt before the
"Three Fates." . . . They are only three women
seated, but they seem to be taking part in
something of enormous import that we do not see.*

Three Goddesses or *Three Fates* from east
pediment of Parthenon, 438-432 B.C.

23

The "*Victory of Samothrace*"
voluptuously shows herself, nude
beneath the thinly pasted veil of
draperies. . . . Place it in your mind,
upon a golden shore, whence, beneath
the olive branches, you may see the
blue and shining sea cradling white
islands! Antique marbles need the full
light of day. In our museums they are
deadened by too heavy shadows.

Victory of Samothrace, c. 190 B.C.

Behold the marvel of marvels! This
work is the expression of the greatest
antique inspiration; it is
voluptuousness regulated by restraint;
it is the joy of life cadenced, moderated
by reason. . . . The artists in those days
had eyes to see, while those of today
are blind; this is all the difference. The
Greek women were beautiful, but their
beauty lived above all in the minds of
the sculptors who carved them.

Venus de Milo, Second Century B.C.

This is the absolute empire of supreme elegance. No vain confusion here, no exaggeration or inflation. And to think that this monument is attributed to barbaric times! . . . However naïve the pedants may judge an analogy between the Gothic church and the northern forests—which were never very far from this cathedral and furnished it with so many materials—that analogy imposes itself upon my mind. I am absolutely convinced that the forests inspired the architect. The builder heard the voice of nature.

Cathedral at Amiens, begun 1220

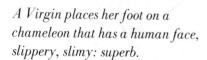

A Virgin places her foot on a chameleon that has a human face, slippery, slimy: superb.

Virgin of the Straight Folds, Cathedral at Amiens, 1220-1238

Why are our Gothic cathedrals so beautiful? It is because in the human images which adorn their portals you can discover a trace of the divine love. Those gentle craftsmen of the Middle Ages saw infinite goodness shining everywhere. And, with their charming simplicity, they have thrown reflections of this loving kindness even on the faces of their demons, to whom they have lent a kindly malice and an air almost of relationship to the angels.

Last Judgment, Amiens portal sculpture, 1220-1238

Donatello was also a student of nature, and how varied he is: more so than Michelangelo. . . . [Michelangelo] took entire figures from Donatello, besides using a certain movement of the wrist and foot, common to the latter. . . . The "St. George" of Donatello is all there is of Italian art, its sum and flower—an angel.

Donatello: *St. George*, c. 1415-1417

All Michelangelo's statues are so constrained by agony that they seem to wish to break themselves. They all seem ready to succumb to the pressure of despair which fills them. . . . If we seek the spiritual significance of . . . Michelangelo, we shall find that his sculpture expressed restless energy, the will to act without the hope of success —the martyrdom of the creature tormented by unrealizable aspirations. . . . The soul thrown back upon itself, suffering, disgust of life, contention against the bonds of matter—such are the elements of his inspiration.

Michelangelo: *Pietà*, c. 1550

Nature, by a divine law, tends constantly toward the best, tends ceaselessly toward perfection. . . . There exists a Northern type, to which many Frenchwomen belong. In this type the hips are strongly developed and the shoulders are narrow; it is this structure that you observe, for example, in the nymphs of Jean Goujon.

Jean Goujon: *Nymph* for Fontaine des Innocents, Paris, 1548-1549

We call ugly whatever suggests the idea of suffering. But let a great artist make use of one of these uglinesses, instantly it is transfigured; with a touch of his wand he has turned it into beauty; it is alchemy; it is enchantment! . . . When Puget swelled the muscles of his heroes, this great French master polished a facet of our national soul: heroism.

Pierre Puget: Caryatid for City Hall, Toulon, c. 1655

I have the greatest admiration for the art of the 18th Century; all the artists of that time took part in something good. But to the art of his time Clodion added something personal; his forms are a bit facile but supple and of such decorative prettiness, such seductive charm!

Claude Michel (called Clodion): *Cupid and Psyche*, late 18th Century

Observation of Voltaire gave the character of the statue by Houdon. It gave him the precise movement of the whole and that astonishing grasp of the hands on the arms of the chair. Houdon saw, understood, was able to translate, and made a masterpiece.

Jean-Antoine Houdon: *Voltaire*, c. 1781

II

Voyages of Discovery

The house at No. 3 Rue de l'Arbalète, where François Auguste René Rodin was born on November 12, 1840, was a warren of families of meager means. The flaking building still stands, and the little street itself, narrow and dank, remains one of those pockets of Left Bank Paris that so far have defied change. The district was grubby even in Rodin's childhood. Still, it was not just another nondescript slum. With its cobbled alleys climbing the slope known as the Montagne-Sainte-Geneviève, it was one of the oldest and most colorful sections of the city. Many an artist has been reared in grimmer surroundings.

Since early medieval times the quarter had seen students from the Sorbonne rubbing shoulders with every sort of artisan and worker. It had housed poets in poverty, witnessed upheavals at the university, and echoed to the mingled sounds of convent bells, craftsmen's hammers and peddlers' cries. The Montagne-Sainte-Geneviève itself gleamed with the Gothic tracery of the shrines of Sainte-Geneviève and Saint-Séverin, the flamboyant Renaissance façade of Saint-Étienne-du-Mont, the pomp of the high dome of the Panthéon—the monument to France's great. By the time of Rodin's youth, the part of the quarter in which he lived, known to its inhabitants as "the Mouffe," after its main street, the Rue Mouffetard, had become an enclave of small storekeepers and junk dealers. Yet all that Rodin saw around him helped provide an education —the shopkeepers' stalls no less than the monuments, the pulse of the city along with the aura of history. The vibrant world of his native Paris gave him, as he once remarked, *"millions de pensées"*—millions of thoughts.

Rodin's parents were recent arrivals in a migration from the provinces that was continually changing the character of Paris. They were above workingman status, although not quite bourgeoisie. The father, Jean-Baptiste, the son of a cotton seller, had come from a small town in Normandy to advance his fortunes, but all he achieved was a clerkship in the Paris police department, followed by a minor post at a Paris prison. Eventually he was promoted to the rank of inspector, only to be pensioned off soon thereafter at half pay at the age of 59. When Auguste,

These pages from a Rodin sketchbook show studies he made in 1857, his last year at art school. He probably based them on plaster casts of classical statuary or on prints after ancient subjects, standard fare for students in Rodin's youth. Although gifted enough to win a school prize for his drawing, Rodin supplemented his classroom training by visiting museums and print collections and observing and then later sketching from memory the life around him.

Although their life was hard, Marie and Jean-Baptiste Rodin were still vigorous in their fifties when their young artisan son, Auguste, painted their portraits *(above)*. These oils and the bust of his father below are among Rodin's earliest efforts at portraiture, but they clearly evoke the senior Rodin's strong-mindedness and his wife's somewhat dour countrywoman's temperament.

in one of his first attempts at portraiture, painted his father the year before his retirement, the canvas showed a deep-browed face with an almost patrician nose. Rodin evidently indulged in some filial flattery; actually his father appears to have been a hard-bitten countryman of limited intelligence. Whatever qualities Auguste inherited from his paternal side seem to have consisted chiefly of a handsome brow, a hearty physique and an urge for money.

Rodin's maternal forebears were industrious peasant folk from Lorraine, on the Franco-German border. (Their name, Cheffer, suggests a French variation of the German Schaefer.) Some of them prospered in Paris; one Cheffer became an engraver, another a designer, a third the head of a printing shop. Marie Cheffer Rodin herself was doomed to a lifetime of struggle; her husband's pay of 1,800 francs a year was barely enough to cover the family needs. Auguste's older sister, Maria, had to take in sewing and on occasion hire herself out as a domestic.

The Cheffers and the Rodins grew into a tightly knit clan whose bonds were strengthened by religion. Jean-Baptiste served as a lay brother of the Order of the Christian Doctrine, while his wife and her sister Thérèse were also ardent Roman Catholics. The family's devotional bent required Catholic schooling for young Auguste. But in three years of primary education at the hands of monks he learned little of spelling or the intricacies of French syntax, with which he was to wrestle ever after. He did learn something else on his own. "As far back as I can remember," he recalled, "I drew." A grocer at whose shop his mother traded wrapped purchases in pages torn from illustrated journals; the pictures, which Auguste copied at home, were his first subjects. At 10 he was packed off to the city of Beauvais, where his father's brother ran a small intermediate school. He hated the routine ("I always felt that I was being held a prisoner") and at 13 returned to his home, a dropout interested only in drawing.

Rodin's frustration and failure to adjust at school may have been caused in part by a physical handicap of which he was not then aware. He was seriously nearsighted and probably found it difficult to see the blackboard. His faulty eyesight may also have influenced his choice of the field of sculpture, in which he could work with the tactile, the plastic, the near at hand.

Beauvais was his last contact with formal schooling. His family was short on resources, higher education was out of the question, and it was decided that he should take up a trade. His father was opposed to his ambition to become an artisan in the field of design, but relented when Auguste's sister Maria pleaded his cause. He was entered in the government's vocational school for applied arts and decoration—the Petite École, as it was called, in contrast to the Grande École, the higher school of the fine arts. The Petite École was chiefly a training ground for commercial draftsmen and *practiciens*—cutters and finishers of work in stone. It was there, from 14 to 17, that Rodin obtained "the only instruction of my life."

At the Petite École, students spent their time copying the work of 18th Century decorators and ornamental painters—among them the celebrated François Boucher—who had flourished at the time the school was founded. Fortunately, however, the faculty included an original and enterprising teacher, Horace Lecoq de Boisbaudran, who influenced a whole generation of aspiring artists to do more than imitate. Lecoq de Boisbaudran had a teaching system that he described in a tract called *Training of Graphic Memory and the Forming of an Artist.* Combining precise study of a subject with freedom from rote in reproducing it, the method required a pupil to observe a plaster cast or an old engraving, for example, with utmost diligence. But when the time came to draw such an object, he had to do so from memory, sometimes days after it had been removed from his sight. He was also told to observe life outside the studio, fix images from nature in his mind, then come back and draw them. In this way the student learned to rely on his own responses. Lecoq de Boisbaudran was a magisterial man who strode among his pupils using the tip of his pocketknife to point out flaws in their work. Some academicians deplored his departures from conventional teaching methods, but students flocked to him. The etcher Alphonse Legros and the sculptor Jules Dalou were classmates of Rodin who achieved early fame; some years later the American James McNeill Whistler became another follower. Young Rodin found his first inspiration in Lecoq de Boisbaudran. To couple tradition with spontaneity, to work both from nature and from memory, was an approach that became an essential part of Rodin's art.

It was perhaps Lecoq de Boisbaudran who aroused Rodin's ambition to become something more than a craftsman, although that possibility then seemed an unfulfillable dream. Painting attracted him but he lacked money to buy paints; he could afford only drawing paper and pencils. Obviously, given his family's circumstances, he had to get out and make a living. Still he worked hard at his studies, an intense, troubled youth, little given to relaxation. He spent his mornings at the school; then, after lunching on a roll or a bar of chocolate, he passed his afternoons sketching sculptures at the Louvre or studying in the print rooms of the Bibliothèque Impériale (where the librarians withheld their choicest volumes from him because of his shabby clothes). In the evening he attended a free course in drawing from the nude given at the Gobelin tapestry works; after that, he drew from memory at home, following Lecoq de Boisbaudran's principles. He also tried to enlarge his general education, attending lectures in history and literature given at the Collège de France to make up for what he had missed. He immersed himself in the works of Victor Hugo, in the poets Alfred de Musset and Alphonse Lamartine, in Dante, Vergil and Homer—the beginning of a lifetime love of literature.

Then, at 17, having won a first prize in modeling in clay at the Petite École and a second in drawing, Rodin was encouraged to try for the Grande École des Beaux-Arts. His father at first objected, but yielded after a recommendation from a leading sculptor, Hippolyte Maindron; his sister Maria, the one confidante at home to his dawning aspirations, took a job to help pay his expenses. Rodin applied and was accepted as a drawing student but was turned down in three successive competitions for a place as a sculpture student. Since virtually anyone with a modicum of ability was accepted, his failure came as a blow. Almost from the moment he had entered the Petite École he had fallen in love with sculpture. "I felt as though I had landed in heaven," he recalled of his introduction to modeling clay. His rejection appears to have been caused less by doubts about his competence than by a certain disdain among the Grande École judges for the light, decorative 18th Century style he had learned at the Petite École; they were wedded to the solemnities of Neoclassicism.

The humiliation not only threw Rodin on his own but made him think about his future. He was not totally dismayed; a drawing he made of himself about this time shows an unsmiling but determined face. There had to be a way ahead for him outside the Beaux-Arts school. Rude and Carpeaux—whose work he much admired—had achieved success without subscribing to its canons. On the other hand, to be a Beaux-Arts graduate was, for most artists, the road to recognition and commissions. On balance, Rodin's rejection as a sculpture student helped to form a personality both adventurous and, for a time, uncertain. For years he was unsure as to where his future might lie, and behaved under a compulsion to learn everything, try anything. This roving led him to test any style or approach that attracted him—a catholic experiment, but one that also kept him from achieving coherence or discipline in his work.

After his third rejection by the Grande École, he set out to support himself. Working at home, he had already fashioned simple clay models of ornaments, such as mantelpiece figurines, that he hawked to silversmiths and decorators in the Mouffe. He now began to work for large commercial designers—at less than five francs a day—mixing plaster, removing mold marks from casts, occasionally making a simple ornament on his own. He labored on ornamental masonry for a contractor, on bric-a-brac for a decorator, on earrings and belt buckles for a jeweler. Soon he was turning out coquettish 18th Century-style nymphs, cupids and masks of gods for the bourgeoisie whose tastes he despised. It became apparent that he was a young man of considerable virtuosity. He could, with equal facility, produce a design for a *trompe l'oeil* ceiling, a caryatid for a theater or a lively chimney ornament for a music hall. He later dismissed these works as "sins of my youth," but he went at them with extraordinary exuberance. Rodin, destined to become known as one of the most serious of sculptors, a man of great force but little levity, also had in him from the outset a love of play, of artifice, of charm and elegance of gesture.

Clearly, he was propelled by two contrasting drives—that of the impassioned seeker of art and that of the craftsman chiefly out to advance his dexterity. He spent years trying to reconcile the two, for a long time unsuccessfully. The need to earn a living played a large part in this, but not the only one: while one side of him deplored the trivia, the other took pride in his skill. He devoted more than a decade and a half to figurines, bric-a-brac, small portrait busts. The work grew increasingly accomplished, but it was still trivia.

As this locket photograph reveals, Rodin and his only sister, Maria, bore a striking resemblance. In many ways they were alike in character, too; both were industrious and capable of intense emotion. Maria, two years older than Rodin, was an unselfish, levelheaded girl. Her virtues so impressed the Sisters of the Doctrine, who educated her, that they hoped she would one day be a teacher. She joined their order—after a broken love affair—but was still a novice when she contracted peritonitis and died following an operation.

For a time even this career seemed doomed by a personal tragedy that all but overwhelmed Rodin when he was 22. His sister Maria, to whom he was deeply devoted, died under circumstances for which he blamed himself. She had fallen in love with one of his fellow students, and had been jilted for another woman. Strictly reared, austere by nature, Maria entered a convent, only to die of peritonitis before taking her final vows. Rodin was anguished, evidently seized with a profound sense of guilt because it was through him that she had met her faithless suitor. Utterly shaken, he decided to abandon art. He abruptly quit his decorative work and entered the Order of the Fathers of the Very Holy Sacrament as a novice. At Christmas 1862 Rodin was serving Mass in a white robe.

Father Pierre-Julien Eymard, founder of the Order of the Fathers of the Very Holy Sacrament, became Rodin's adviser and confessor when, grief-stricken at the death of his sister Maria, he entered the Order as a novice. Father Eymard encouraged Rodin to pursue his true vocation and considerately assigned him a small shed on the monastery grounds for use as a studio. Later the bearded young sculptor completed the bust of Father Eymard shown below.

From the outset, however, it seemed clear that he was not intended for the monastic life. Fortunately the head of his Order, Father Eymard, was a discerning as well as devout man (he was later canonized) and he encouraged his novice to go on sculpting. Brother Augustin made a bust of Father Eymard himself, and a remarkable achievement it was—an affectionate yet searching study of a gifted and knowing man of God. Father Eymard, however, objected to what he called the "hornlike" treatment of his hair and would not pay Rodin for copies he had ordered of it. Perhaps the effort persuaded Rodin to reconsider his true calling. Before many months he abandoned the surplice for the smock and was back at his cupids and ornaments. A photograph of him at the time shows a deeply perturbed young man. Religion was not to figure importantly again in his life.

At 23, Rodin was earning enough to rent his first studio and free his family's flat of the mess and disorder of his job work. For 120 francs a year he got an unheated, drafty stable on the Rue Lebrun, beyond the Latin Quarter. It was, Rodin recalled, "glacially cold" and "cluttered with works in progress," which he tried vainly to protect against the effects of temperature extremes. "Since I didn't have the money to have them cast, each day I lost precious time covering my clay with wet cloths. Despite that, at every turn I had accidents from the effects of cold and heat. Entire sections detached themselves—heads, arms, knees, chunks of torsos fell off; I found them in pieces on the tiles that covered the floor. . . . You could not believe what I lost in that way." His plaint suggests that he was working not just on commercial items but on studies and figures for his own satisfaction, although virtually nothing is known about these "lost" objects. He was obviously sculpting many heads, but the only completed work that survives is a bust of his father. Modeled in clay and later cast in bronze, it shows the increasing command of style that characterized the bust of Father Eymard, but again Rodin ran into an unfavorable reaction from his sitter. Father Eymard had objected to the overemphasis on his hair; Rodin's father, who had a luxuriant growth and a full beard, was annoyed that his son sculpted him almost hairless. The effect of the taut, naked skin lends the bust a classical power, but Jean-Baptiste Rodin did not fancy himself as a Roman senator.

When not at work in the studio, the young artist made efforts to improve his skills, training his hand by drawing such events as the horse auctions held on the Boulevard Saint-Marcel. He also attended a class at the Museum of Natural History conducted by the well-known sculptor of animals Antoine-Louis Barye. The course included the study of live animals in motion, observed at the adjoining menagerie in the Jardin des Plantes, where Barye taught Rodin and his other students to look for intense, violent muscular movement (the zoo had also been a favorite haunt of Delacroix, past master of stirring movement, animal and human). Rodin appears to have enjoyed himself under Barye's tutelage. He and his fellow students took over a room in the basement of the Museum where they modeled lions' paws and studied animal skeletons, adjourning after their studies for glasses of wine in nearby cafés.

He was also making some more important contacts. Shortly after renting his studio he was invited to join a lively circle formed by a number of prominent men interested in advancing the applied arts—the Union Centrale des Arts Décoratifs, it was called. At its meetings and dinners Rodin encountered such dignitaries as Ingres, Delacroix, Alexandre Dumas père, Théophile Gautier and the sculptor Carpeaux. Young artists were invited to make their entrance into the group showing the best they could produce: Rodin arrived one evening with a cast of his bust of Father Eymard under his arm and won warm applause.

In 1864 Rodin made three moves of great importance for the future. He acquired a mistress, Rose Beuret, who was to bear him a son and remain with him for the rest of his life despite the intervention of many other women along the way. He took a designer's job with France's most successful mass-producer of *objects d'art*, Albert-Ernest Carrier-Belleuse—an association that absorbed a considerable part of his energies over the next decade and a half. And on his own he sculpted the head known as *The Man with the Broken Nose (page 77)*, of which he himself declared, "It determined all my future work."

The subject was an elderly neighborhood odd-jobman known only as "Bibi." His features were furrowed and battered but, in Rodin's words he "had a fine head, belonged to a fine race—in form—no matter if he was brutalized." What Rodin had in mind for Bibi was a character portrayal based not on convention but on his own close observation. The result was daring in every sense—in the subject Rodin had chosen to portray, in the stark yet compassionate treatment and, above all, in the unusual technique employed.

Sculpting Bibi, Rodin dispensed with the tradition that required a bust to have a poised frontal look, supporting shoulders and a formal base. Nothing was here but the head itself, cocked forward, leaving the eyes in shadow. None of the smoothness and symmetry of conventional sculpture marked the work. It was, instead, a mass of broken facets, innumerable ridges and hollows that here caught an expressive flicker of light, there remained shaded. Rodin seemed to have pounded his material, rather than modeled it, producing an effect that had all the raw violence of an eruption. As Rodin saw him Bibi was no obsequious handyman. "This face," wrote Rainer Maria Rilke four decades later, "had not only been touched by life; it had been permeated through and through by it."

There were a number of sources from which Rodin may have drawn inspiration for his portrait of Bibi. Among the Louvre's treasures were sculptures from the declining years of ancient Greece, the Hellenistic period, when artists worked with special ferocity; they produced deeply carved faces that expressed human passion rather than the semidivine serenity of classical Greek sculpture. Also in Paris, in a private collection, was a bust of Michelangelo by his disciple Daniele da Volterra; it showed an aging man seared by struggle and, like Bibi, possessed of a broken nose. Despite the gulf between the two subjects, Rodin seems to have been haunted by the *Michelangelo* when he produced the bust of Bibi as a kind of allegory of the endurance of mankind.

Rodin never lessened his commitment to portrait sculpture as a means of psychological revelation. One day many years later he discussed this subject with his friend the critic Paul Gsell, as they paused in the Louvre before Houdon's study of Voltaire *(page 35)*. "What a marvel it is!" Rodin said. "It is the personification of malice. See! his sidelong glance seems watching some adversary. He has the pointed nose of a fox. . . . You can see it quiver! And the mouth—what a triumph! It is framed by two furrows of irony. It seems to mumble sarcasms."

Gsell remarked that Rodin seemed to think resemblance a very important quality in portraiture. Rodin replied that it was indispensable, but added: "If the artist only reproduces superficial features as photography does, if he copies the lineaments of a face exactly, without reference to character, he deserves no admiration. The resemblance which he ought to obtain is that of the soul; that alone matters; it is that which the sculptor or painter should seek beneath the mask of features. In a word, all the features must be expressive . . . in the revelation of a conscience."

"But doesn't it sometimes happen," Gsell asked, "that the face contradicts the soul?"

"Never."

"Have you forgotten the precept of La Fontaine, 'One should not judge people by appearances'?"

"That maxim," Rodin declared, "is only addressed to superficial observers. For appearances may deceive their hasty examination. La Fontaine writes that the little mouse took the cat for the kindest of creatures, but he speaks of a little mouse—that is to say, of a scatterbrain who lacked critical faculty. The appearance of a cat would warn whoever studied it attentively that there was cruelty hidden under that sleepiness."

A true portrait, Rodin summed up, was in effect a biography, and it was the artist's role "to show the truth, even beneath dissimulation." To do so required penetration and intelligence. For an artist so endowed, "the line of a forehead, the least lifting of a brow, the flash of an eye all reveal to him the secrets of the heart." Everything he perceived in the human physiognomy, indeed, served to help "read the soul within."

T*he Man with the Broken Nose* was Rodin's first masterpiece, although it won recognition only slowly. Shortly after he had worked up the head in clay, he decided to cast it in plaster and submit it to the Salon of 1864. Then calamity struck. One winter day, in the freezing temperature of his studio, the head came apart and the rear half broke off. Rodin nevertheless decided to cast the frontal portion and submit it to the Salon—to make his first appearance on the Paris artistic scene with a masklike fragment. The Salon jury summarily rejected it. The head of Bibi returned to Rodin's studio, there to remain until several years later, when one of Rodin's students, Jules Desbois, saw the cast in a corner and received permission to borrow it to make a copy. The next day he took it to show to his classmates at the Grande École. "Look at this superb piece of antique sculpture," he told them. "I've just discovered it at a dealer's." As they stood around admiringly Desbois angrily burst forth: "The man who made it, whose name is Rodin, failed three times to enter the school, and the work you take to be antique was refused by the Salon."

Rodin's "antique" was also his first revolution, his first major challenge to the canons of the artistic establishment. The Salon's rebuff did not unduly upset him. He was in the first flush of his liaison with Rose Beuret, whom he had met by chance in a confectionery shop. She was working as a seamstress near the Théâtre des Gobelins, where Rodin was producing gaudy façade decorations. Daughter of a vineyardist, Rose could barely write, but she was 20, petite and pretty, with the engaging air of a country girl. Her life with Rodin was to be a peculiar odyssey. She became not only his mistress and model but his faithful housekeeper and studio helper and slave, tending his clays diligently with moist cloths and even buttoning his boots. Some of his friends scorned her. One described her as "a little washerwoman" who had "absolutely no communication" with Rodin—except, presumably, in bed. In later years she lapsed into embitterment and freakish behavior and was often banished from the master's presence when distinguished guests were present. She was, he had decided, "too much of a savage."

Yet when both were young, life even in meager circumstances was gay. They lived together at first in the unheated Rue Lebrun stable-studio, where he made a number of busts of her; in one, *Mignon (page 82)*, she appears as a pensive charmer. She also posed for a life-sized figure entitled *Bacchante*, but it was later accidentally smashed. For two years they kept their life secret from his parents, but in 1866 she bore him a son, and Rodin thought he had better break the news. Oddly—he was perhaps still an uncertain bohemian—he did not do so directly, but through an intermediary, his aunt Thérèse Cheffer. His mother could not quite understand why he had not married the girl, but accepted her nonetheless. (One malicious acquaintance remarked that he had fallen so in love with his *Mignon* that he could not marry its sitter.) Soon Auguste and Rose moved from his studio to a flat in Montmartre where he drew her cradling the baby, who had been baptized Auguste but listed on the records under his mother's name of Beuret *("père inconnu")*. Little Auguste also became an occasional model when there was call for a cupid. Life was looking up; Rodin was working regularly, Rose was a good cook, and on Sundays there were trips into the countryside with a full hamper and plenty of wine.

Their fortunes had begun to improve when Rodin joined the atelier of the sculptor-decorator Carrier-Belleuse and started receiving regular wages. He fitted in naturally, for he and his employer shared many ideas. Like Rodin, Carrier-Belleuse had a taste in decoration for 18th Century airiness rather than the accepted Neoclassical stupor. And again like Rodin, he was endlessly versatile, whether producing a bust of George Sand or Emperor Napoleon III, or designing an ornamental clock or chandelier. Nevertheless Rodin, who was one of a large troop of draftsmen, molders, finishers and casters in Carrier-Belleuse's employ, had a decidedly ambivalent attitude toward his employer. After he no longer needed the work, he declared: "Nothing I ever did for him interested me." In a more generous vein, he once asserted that Carrier-Belleuse had valid artistic instincts.

As one of Carrier-Belleuse' chief assistants, Rodin received a number of diverting assignments, such as producing the roof decorations for the mansion of the Marquise de Païva, one of the reigning hostesses of Paris. The house, on the Champs Élysées, was the scene of magnificent receptions attended by the leading literary and political figures of the city. Carrier-Belleuse also entrusted Rodin with the adornment of the staircases and doorways of other opulent Paris houses. The work was a distinct advance over his humbler labors of previous years, and economic security seemed assured.

Then in 1870 came the shock of the Franco-Prussian War. The French were ill-prepared; the Prussians were magnificently equipped, trained and led. It took them only the summer of 1870 to cross the Rhine, subdue Alsace-Lorraine and lay siege to Paris. Rodin was called up to serve in the National Guard. Soon discharged because of his poor eyesight, he was at a loss to support his family. The call for decorators' services had dwindled. Carrier-Belleuse had prudently left Paris at the outbreak of the war, responding to a call from neutral and prosperous Belgium to provide ornamental sculpture for the Brussels stock exchange. Happily for Rodin, the contract was a large one, and Carrier-Belleuse not only enlisted a number of Brussels craftsmen but asked his unemployed former assistant to join him.

Rodin spent the next six years abroad—years that marked a turning both in his career and in the history of France. Even before he left Paris Napoleon III was deposed, the Second Empire collapsed, the Third Republic that was destined to endure until World War II came shakily into being, Paris fell to the Prussians, and an uneasy peace was concluded. There is no evidence that Rodin paid much notice to the turmoil that beset his native land. To the end of his life he remained uninterested in politics.

The years away from Paris began badly, for the relationship with Carrier-Belleuse soon deteriorated. Socially amiable but imperious with subordinates, Carrier-Belleuse had a long-standing habit of encouraging assistants to make small figures that, slightly retouched, he sold as his own handiwork. He did this with some of Rodin's work, but when Rodin tried to market some mantelpiece figurines that he had made on his own time, his annoyed employer fired him. Rose, left behind in Paris until Rodin could become established in Brussels, received such notes as this: "My darling angel, I write you in the depths of despair . . . things looked as if they would work out; now I don't care about anything. Write at once; I'll be able to send you a little money. If only I may be able to press you again to my heart, Rose!"

After months of unemployment, Rodin went into partnership with another former Carrier-Belleuse assistant who had a contract to execute sculptures and bas-reliefs for a number of public buildings in Brussels. With this encouraging prospect Rose joined her lover, leaving young Auguste in the care of the ever-helpful Aunt Thérèse Cheffer. Life in

This 15-inch statuette by Rodin's longtime employer, Albert-Ernest Carrier-Belleuse, suggests the reason for his commercial success: he knew what the public wanted in the way of sculpture. The French bourgeoisie liked to clutter their apartments with such small *objets d'art*. Made of bronze and mounted on onyx or marble bases, they usually featured classical figures acting out mythological tales or sentimental vignettes of everyday life. In this work, displaying a lightness of touch and gay charm that Rodin admired, Carrier-Belleuse sculpted a scene that was titillating yet presentable: her body provocatively arched, a nymph raises clenched fists in one last struggle against her captor, who tenderly gazes at such adorable resistance.

exile, even in a one-room flat, proved idyllic. On weekends Rose and Auguste walked and picnicked among the beeches in the nearby forest of Soignes. Rodin delighted in its austerity, so different from the lush forests around Paris. He took along paintbox and brushes and produced a series of oils of the copses and clearings and windmills of rural Brabant, much in the manner of Corot and the Barbizon landscapists. The paintings were warm and peaceful, reflecting both Rodin's new-found composure and his great skill with the brush; had not his fame as a sculptor overtaken them they might be more widely known today.

A variety of commissions earned him a modest living. He made the

Rodin's bust of his employer, finished in
1882, shows the long hair and studied
dishabille that Carrier-Belleuse affected to
advertise himself as artist-entrepreneur. Like
Rodin, Carrier-Belleuse was a poor boy who
served a lengthy apprenticeship in studios
that manufactured ornamental art. He went
on to become one of France's most popular
sculptor-decorators and eventually a director
of the Sèvres porcelain works. He employed
Rodin in his own workshop and at Sèvres and
in gratitude Rodin produced this portrait,
later used to grace its subject's tomb.

models for 10 carved stone caryatids—three of them more than six feet
high—for mansions on Brussels' patrician Boulevard Anspach, and designed groups of cupids for the façade of the Palais des Académies. He
did much of the work on a flamboyant civic monument in Antwerp
—an immense pile of assorted figures in heroic attitudes, with busts,
masks, and a female torchbearer on top of the heap—all intended to
honor a past burgomaster. Fortunately for Rodin's future reputation
he was not asked to sign the work.

By 1875 he had saved enough money to undertake what he knew
would be his great adventure. Like so many artists before him he de-

Rodin fashioned the terra-cotta *Vase of the Titans (above)* when he worked in Carrier-Belleuse' studio factory. In the sketch design that he was given to follow, an almost languid grace characterized the figures, but Rodin was fresh from a trip to Italy and much under the spell of Michelangelo. As a preliminary, he presented his boss with the studies at left, their muscular contortions conveying a sense of strain that recalls Michelangelo's figures. Evidently Carrier-Belleuse liked the revised concept, for he signed the base of the finished work and put it on the market as his own.

cided on a pilgrimage to Italy to encounter Renaissance art at first hand. He left Rose in Brussels and set forth on a journey into the past that would shape his future. Traveling in part on foot, he wrote her of his southward progress: "I must tell you that there is a sausage I got at Pontarlier that is beginning to give me trouble; I thought one couldn't eat in Italy and I got this as a final reinforcement. Yet I am eating well now and drinking amply to your good health." Then, safely across the Alps, from Genoa: "Artichokes and petits-pois here (and very pretty women, Rosette)." From Florence, the hour of impact: "From the moment I arrived, I began to study Michelangelo . . . and I believe this

Rodin's figures for his *Vase of the Titans* (*preceding pages*) show a debt to Michelangelo's nude youths above. Called *ignudi*, they are two of many such figures in the frescoes on the Sistine Chapel ceiling. Rodin never again relied so directly on Michelangelo, although for a long time he continued to view himself as a spiritual disciple of the Florentine master.

great magician will reveal some of his secrets to me. . . . I've made sketches in the evening in my room, not of his works, but of figures I have imagined and elaborated in order to understand his technique. Well, I think I have succeeded and that they have that nameless something which he alone could give."

Rodin later recalled that the tombs Michelangelo carved for the Medici family impressed him more than anything he had ever seen, and that he had felt compelled to copy the great Florentine. At the same time he found himself wholly disconcerted by Michelangelo's works: "They constantly contradicted all those truths that I believed that I had definitely acquired. 'Look here,' I said to myself, 'why this incurvation of the body, this raised hip, this lowered shoulder?' I was very much upset. And yet Michelangelo could not have been mistaken!"

What he was facing was a master who also had struck out on his own, leaning on what he liked best in the past—Donatello, the ancients, even taking entire figures from them—yet subjecting them all to his own judgment and experience of life. To feel intensely, and to be fearless and unbounded in conveying one's feeling—this was the essence that Rodin found in the man who liberated him. "It was he who reached out his mighty hand to me. It was over this bridge that I passed from one world [that of the French Écoles] to another." This was, one could say, Rodin's moment of truth.

Curiously, he also found in Michelangelo—the epitome of the High Renaissance—"the last and greatest of the Gothics . . . the culmination of all Gothic thought." What struck Rodin was Michelangelo's concern with spiritual meanings. The strains and exaggerations of many of Michelangelo's forms, the unfinished state of others, the awesome gesture of the *Moses*, the brooding melancholy of the allegorical *Dawn* and *Dusk* on the tomb of Lorenzo de' Medici, suggesting the passage and corruption of time—all these aroused Rodin, who saw in the figures "the martyrdom of the creature tormented by unrealizable aspirations."

Rodin's hegira lasted three months, taking him also to Naples and Venice at a cautious outlay of no more than five francs a day. When he rejoined Rose he was in a fever of excitement. Having found his affinity for Michelangelo, Rodin now tackled the problem of how to draw on his example, not just copy from it. He began work on a full-scale figure that, while showing Michelangelo's influence, was quite unlike anything Rodin had actually seen in Italy. The piece, a male nude destined to become famous as *The Age of Bronze (pages 78 and 79)*, was freestanding, both literally and figuratively, and it signaled the end of Rodin's 20-year apprenticeship in art. It also caused a major scandal.

For more than a year, between ornamental commissions, Rodin employed Private Auguste Neyt, a young soldier of the Brussels garrison and a man of extraordinary physique, to model for the form that had dawned in his mind. For several hours a day Private Neyt stood and walked in Rodin's studio in the city's outskirts while the sculptor made numberless sketches and clay models of him at rest and in motion, both in sunlight and candlelight. Perhaps no such intense study of the anatomy of a living figure had ever been made. Whether Rodin had a particular theme in prospect has since been widely argued, and he certainly encouraged debate by the successive titles he gave the work: *The Vanquished, The Man Who Awakens to Nature, Primeval Man* and, finally, *The Age of Bronze*. Those who saw the figure under its first title assumed that he was memorializing the French military disaster of 1870-1871 ("a glorification of a vanquished hero," presumably to rise again, as one biographer put it). Later Rodin said that he had in mind "man arising from nature" and perhaps the final title, *The Age of Bronze*, confirms that idea: it was in the Bronze Age that men discarded primitive stone tools and began to work with metal, and it was also in the Bronze Age that writing came into relatively widespread use. Still later, Rodin asserted that he had had in mind "just a simple piece of sculpture without reference to subject." Yet he never worked without thought of "subject." Perhaps in this case Rodin's theme, consciously or not, was himself, and the work was an allegory of his own awakening.

In posture *The Age of Bronze* recalls Michelangelo's *Dying Slave*, a large marble nude intended for the tomb of Pope Julius II. There is the same multiple twist, or *contrapposto*, of the body to convey a sense of motion: the knees are bent, the head is forward, the arm upraised in evident emotion. At the same time the subject seems to be in a trance. But there the similarity ends. The *Slave* is wearily sinking; Rodin's youth seems on the point of awakening, soon to stride forth with fresh energy.

Rodin's work was first exhibited in Brussels in 1877. It was a sensation. To observers accustomed to taking sculpture as a formal commentary on life, here was something that looked all too much like life itself. Anything so lifelike had to be a fraud, and indeed the artist was charged by some critics with *surmoulage*—encasing his living model in a mold of plaster and casting directly from it without any creative work of his own.

Soon there were other attacks in Brussels, and then in Paris, where Rodin sent the figure. "Is this the statue of a sleepwalker?" one critic asked. "Incomprehensible," wrote another, "why does this little man grasp his head? Why do his eyes appear to be blinded? Why, anyway, does he not stand straight on his legs?" Still another critic dismissed it as "an astonishingly accurate copy of a low type."

No attack hurt Rodin more than the charge of imposture. The 1877 Salon jury had accepted the work by a narrow margin and placed it in an outer hall. As rumors of falsification spread, talk arose of removing it. Salon guards found a placard placed against it by persons unknown reading, "Molded on the body of the model." Rodin was enraged. He dashed off protests to newspapers, had photographs made of Private Neyt to prove that the sculpture differed in many respects from the living body, and demanded an official inquiry and vindication by the Ministry of Fine Arts. Numerous artists rallied to defend his integrity, and soon vindication came. The French government bought a cast of the work for 2,200 francs—the precise amount it had cost Rodin to put it in bronze. No one ever bothered to open the packet of photographs he had prepared. It was really not necessary. He had not "copied," in either a vulgar or a fashionable sense. He had simply learned to see.

Most French sculpture of the 19th Century was locked in the clutches of convention. The ultraconservative Académie des Beaux-Arts set the standards at the annual Salons, and both public and private patrons of art relied on these exhibitions to form their tastes. An artist who won applause at the Salon could count on sales to wealthy buyers and, even more desirable, civic commissions. Opportunities for these projects abounded. Monuments to Heroism filled every square; myriads of Joans of Arc gestured militantly into the air. (At one point the city of Paris considered a 10-year moratorium on statuary because public space had become so crowded.)

With its power to make or break an artist, the Academy grew increasingly intolerant of nonconformity and doctrinaire in its teachings. Students at its schools were told that the art of classical Greece and Rome was the only acceptable example for them to follow. But instead of studying from nature, as the ancients had done, they simply imitated antique art. They were even given a code of "correct" proportions to guide them, and the sculptor who deviated from the ideal was condemned as vulgar.

Still, there were those among Rodin's predecessors and contemporaries who managed to keep their peace with the Academy and yet maintain their individuality. They made their own direct observations of nature and explored a broadened range of human experience. So-called "official" art was at least in part redeemed through their efforts.

Sculpture and the Academy

France's chief monument to the martial spirit adorns the Arc de Triomphe in Paris. More than 36 feet high, the dramatic relief is dominated by a winged goddess urging on her soldiers—young, old, tired, wounded. Rodin greatly admired the dynamism of this work and had it in mind when he created his own monument on the same subject *(page 125)*.

François Rude: *Departure of the Volunteers of 1792 (La Marseillaise)*, 1833-1836

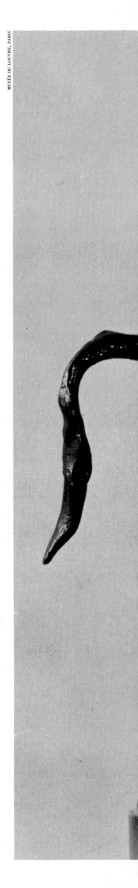

David d'Angers: *Fénelon*, 1827

Along with François Rude, David d'Angers and Antoine-Louis Barye set an example for French sculptors who wished to break the academic mold. David was a portraitist of great verve and perception. He left some 150 busts and 500 portrait medallions, an impressive gallery of the celebrities of his own and earlier times. Above is his study of the 17th Century prelate and unorthodox educational theorist, François Fénelon.

Barye—under whom Rodin briefly studied—was, and remains, unsurpassed as a sculptor of animals. Trained as a metal craftsman, he enjoyed some success at the Salon but had to earn his living producing bronzes of animals for private collectors. Barye's beasts, often shown in combat *(right)*, belie their small size by the sense of colossal power they generate.

54

Antoine-Louis Barye: *Bull Attacked by a Tiger*, date unknown

Antoine-Louis Barye: *Arab Spearing a Lion*, before 1850

Hailed as the "Michelangelo of the menagerie," Barye had such expert knowledge of animal anatomy that he served as professor of animal drawing at the Paris Museum of Natural History. Although his sculptures usually show animals hunting or being hunted, he never saw them in their natural habitats; his observations were based entirely on visits to the Paris zoo. As a result, the works are accurate in every detail of muscle and fur but often present implausible juxtapositions. In the sculpture at the lower right, an Asian orangutan

Antoine-Louis Barye: *Tiger and Civet*, before 1855

Antoine-Louis Barye: *Orangutan Riding a Gnu*, c. 1855

improbably rides a prancing African gnu.

Like his friend the Romantic painter Eugène Delacroix, Barye was concerned not with literal natural history but with the drama of conflict. He also shared Delacroix's fascination with exotic locales, especially North Africa, then a French colony. Barye's *Arab Spearing a Lion (left)* is a small masterpiece of energy and movement. Equally violent and compelling is his *Tiger and Civet (above, top)*. Delacroix once said of Barye: "I wish I could put a twist in a tiger's tail like that man."

Jean-Baptiste Carpeaux: *Ugolino*, 1861

Gnawing his fingers in agony and grief, the imprisoned traitor of Pisa, Ugolino, sits among his dying sons. Based on a story from Dante's *Inferno* that Rodin would also later exploit, the sculpture above *(detail, left)* made the reputation of Jean-Baptiste Carpeaux, a former student of François Rude. If Carpeaux's *Ugolino* group seems indebted to Michelangelo's muscular figures and to the famous Greek statue *Laocoön and His Sons*, the resemblance is understandable. The work was produced in Rome—home of numerous Michelangelos and of the *Laocoön*—while Carpeaux was enjoying the fruits of a scholarship he had won as a student at the École des Beaux-Arts in Paris. At its Roman debut in 1861 *Ugolino* was clamorously praised.

The work stamped its creator as an artist with a flair for the melodramatic. Rodin, who knew him and admired his work, said of him: "Carpeaux loved his art passionately; he expressed it with the heat of an essentially impulsive temperament; he had to the highest pitch a feeling for grandeur."

59

One of the first Establishment sculptors to support Rodin was Alexandre Falguière, a prize winner at the École des Beaux-Arts. In his own work, however, Falguière was not adventurous. He preferred a smooth, idealized rendering of the human body and an anecdotal approach to themes, intended both to please the eye and to satisfy the mind with familiar references. One of his most popular efforts was *The Victor of the Cockfight (right, and detail, left)*, showing a nude youth, presumably running home from the cockpit with his prized bird. The graceful, lithe figure of the boy has some of the delicacy and spirit typical of France's finest art, but it is essentially frivolous and, despite its seeming movement, static. Sentimentality pervades Falguière's *Tarcisius (below)*, a monument to a young early-Christian martyr who was stoned to death. Sculpturally, the work represents a tendency against which Rodin rebelled strongly: it can only be seen and understood satisfactorily from a single viewpoint. In effect, it might as well be a relief, or even a painting, for it does not exist in the three dimensions that sculpture, by definition, demands.

Alexandre Falguière: *The Victor of the Cockfight*, 1864

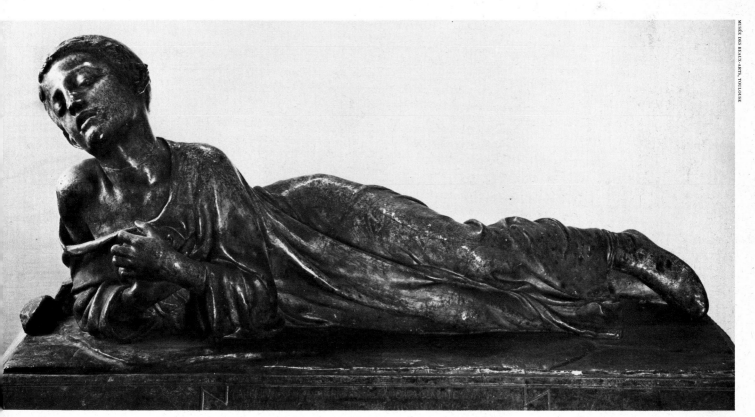

Alexandre Falguière: *Tarcisius*, 1875

Antonin Mercié: *Quand Même*, 1882

Antonin Mercié represented what Rodin detested in art: formularized technique, a stereotyped or sentimentalized depiction of life, and a certain pandering to public taste. The overly theatrical gesture of the dying soldier above plainly betrays the intent of this monument—to elicit a predictable response of tearful chauvinism. The monument is also composed in the strict pyramidal form that the Academy ruled proper.

Jules Dalou's *Triumph of Silenus (right)* may not at first seem superior to the work by Mercié, yet its dynamism of movement and its complex interweaving shapes make it more interesting visually. In both theme and execution it represents a return to the liveliness of the Baroque style and a departure from the rigidities of the academic tradition. Dalou's figures also exude a vitality that helps explain Rodin's high regard for his contemporary.

Jules Dalou: *The Triumph of Silenus*, 1894-1898
LUXEMBOURG GARDENS, PARIS

III

A Rage to Produce

When Rodin returned to Paris in 1877, charges of fakery still raged about his *Age of Bronze*. He was deeply wounded, but not dismayed, telling Rose, "I trust in the power of truth." Confident that he would eventually be vindicated, he was also greatly stimulated by the prospect of resuming life on his home ground. Six years in Brussels had awakened him to the scope of his powers, and he was now ready to realize them. He was 37 and well traveled; the urge to assimilate all that he had learned and to strike out afresh was at its peak. His first two years back in Paris witnessed a tumultuous unleashing of his energies.

A less determined man would have found it difficult to concentrate. The domestic situation Rodin faced when he and Rose settled in a small flat in the Rue Saint-Jacques on the Left Bank was distinctly strained. Misfortune had overtaken the Rodin-Cheffer clan. His mother, who had hoped to see her son properly married, was dead. His father had become blind and senile and was being cared for by his widowed sister-in-law, Rodin's Aunt Thérèse, who also had Rodin's son Auguste in her charge. Now 11, Auguste seemed mentally retarded. Possibly he had suffered a brain injury in a fall from a second-story window; in any event he was slow to understand and capable of only limited effort. Rodin may have suspected even before his departure for Brussels that his son was backward. This would explain, if not excuse, his callous abandonment of the boy for six years, and Rose's acceptance of the separation from her child.

Now, with Brussels behind them, they could no longer avoid their family problems. Both Rodin's son and his dying father joined the ménage, and misery descended upon it. While Rose undertook their care, Rodin remained coldly aloof. He declined to give the boy his family name, just as he failed to give it to his common-law wife of 14 years' standing. He did attempt to give young Auguste some drawing lessons, but otherwise seems to have ignored him. Increasingly he ignored Rose as well; more soothing female company was easy to find in Paris. Rose, little more than a servant, began to move into the background of his life. The signs of humiliation became visible on her face, far different in ex-

The airy, ornamental neo-Baroque style that Rodin learned at the Petite École served him well when he began to try to earn a living. Academicians may not have liked it —they refused Rodin admission to the prestigious Grande École—but the public adored it. Thus Rodin readily found work in the decorative trade, creating statuettes similar to this graceful mother and child, perhaps posed by his mistress Rose and their son.

Young Woman and Child, 1865-1870
RODIN MUSEUM, PARIS

While in the employ of a Parisian sculptor-decorator, Rodin created the bizarre masks above for the façade of the Trocadéro palace, an exhibition hall built for the Paris world's fair of 1878. The Trocadéro's architecture was ersatz Moorish with traces of Roman and Spanish décor, a floridly exotic style that Rodin presumably hoped to enhance by these exuberant faces of fantasy.

pression from the spirited Mignon of their earlier days. When she posed for Rodin now, he produced a bust of a mature woman marked by ordeal. The head was roughly incised and topped by something resembling a helmet. He submitted it to the Ministry of Fine Arts as an image of the noble France of the Third Republic, but it was too grim and stark for official tastes. Rodin then titled it *Bellona*, after the Roman goddess, sister of Mars, and tried to sell it, without success.

His private troubles could not quell his enthusiasm for work; undertakings of every sort absorbed him. A sculptor-decorator named André Laouste hired him to help design a pair of immense tragedy-comedy masks for an arcade outside the new Trocadéro exhibition palace in Paris. Exhibited in plaster under Laouste's name at the Salon of 1878, they won a gold medal; Rodin's own *Man with the Broken Nose*, at last accepted at the Salon that year, won nothing. If he felt any chagrin he concealed it and went off to Nice to collaborate on a huge mask of Neptune for the villa of a reigning soprano. Marseilles was his next stop; precisely what he did there is not known, but he may have worked on ornamental statuary for the Palace of Fine Arts. He hastened next to Strasbourg, where he did some of the decorations for a public building; on a return visit 30 years later he himself could not pick out the building on which he had worked. Along the way he found time to write Rose about the beauty of the women he encountered, adding "don't let that make you cross."

Back in Paris he threw himself energetically into a series of sculpture competitions held by the government. The Third Republic may have differed from the Second Empire in its politics, but it displayed the same zest for erecting monuments. While there were no more competitions for statues of Napoleons I and III and their proconsuls, there was room in ministerial budgets for sculptural homage to worthy intellectuals, revolutionists and even the common soldier.

In various competitions Rodin submitted models for figures of the encyclopedist Denis Diderot and the philosopher Jean-Jacques Rousseau, whose writings had influenced the makers of the Revolution of 1789, and for a figure of a renowned revolutionary general of that period, Lazare Carnot—each time, however, without success. He also entered a contest held by the City of Paris for a memorial to the city's defenders during the Prussian siege of 1871. The terra-cotta model he submitted in 1879 under the title *Call to Arms (page 125)* was a particularly ambitious effort. A wounded warrior, powerfully formed but sinking, is seen being rallied by an anguished winged female (posed by Rose). With its dramatic agitation and pathos, it was reminiscent of Rude's brilliant *La Marseillaise*, which adorns the Arc de Triomphe, a fact that may have given Rodin high hopes for acceptance. Also discernible in it are influences of Michelangelo's rendering of the dead Savior being supported by His mother—the *Pietà* in the Cathedral of Florence *(page 31)*—and of Bernini's visionary Saint Theresa receiving the miraculous gift of divine love in the form of a dart held by an angel. But Rodin's sculpture is far more emotional than the *Pietà*, and far less polished than *The Ecstasy of Saint Theresa*. It is instead marked by the apparent incoherence and broken-surfaced look that were becoming characteristic of Rodin's work. Once again he had defied the rules of academic sculpture. The jury saw none of the work's strength and dismissed it even before it reached the finals in the competition; the award went to a confection by a conservative, Louis Ernest Barrias.

Rodin's rejected entry was not entirely forgotten by French officialdom, however. Many years later, after World War I, it was enlarged in gilded bronze, retitled *Defense of Verdun* and erected on the Verdun battlefield. The one City of Paris commission he did win in the 1870s was for a conventionally posed figure of the 18th Century philosopher Jean Le Rond d'Alembert; it still stands in a niche in the façade of the Hôtel de Ville, the Paris City Hall, noticed by few.

All this was only a small part of what Rodin accomplished between 1877 and 1879. While competing for official commissions he was also working on his own, creating figures that are enduring testaments to his genius. Among the most remarkable are *The Walking Man (page 80)* and *St. John the Baptist Preaching (page 81)*. The first was a study for the second, although in time each came to be recognized as an independent work, landmarks in the development of modern sculpture.

Both, like *The Age of Bronze*, treat the male nude, seen not in a static position but vibrant with stir and motion. Certainly there was nothing new about this. The sculptors of ancient Greece were masters at producing a sense of turbulent movement, as were Donatello, Michelangelo and Bernini. Rodin succeeded in adding another dimension—time. His two figures seem not only in motion but in successive stages of motion; Rodin made sculptural drama out of the simple act of striding. In *The Walking Man*, motion is all we sense, for the figure was left headless and armless: no facial expression or gesture deflects interest from a torso borne ahead on wide-spaced, massive legs, its muscles taut and its weight shifting. The impression of motion is further heightened by the play of light, caught by the hollows and knobs and ridges with which Rodin exuberantly modeled the figure.

In the *St. John*, on the other hand, the figure is complete with expressive head and arms and it is more finished, its modeling far smoother. But the posture, the act of walking, is the same. There are no iconographical symbols to identify the sculpture with Christ's cousin St. John —no sheepskin shirt, no prophetic cross usually associated with the Biblical figure; Rodin's *St. John* is just a naked man with an appealing, mature face, marching forward with an outstretched arm. The title Rodin gave this work suggests religious content, but he may simply have superimposed the title because of his fondness for literary allusions. He himself once described the inspiration for *St. John* in somewhat ambiguous terms. "One morning," he recalled, "someone knocked at the studio door. In came an Italian . . . a peasant from Abruzzi, arrived the night before from his birthplace . . . he had come to offer himself to me as a model. . . . Seeing him, I was seized with admiration: that rough, hairy man, expressing in his bearing and physical strength all the violence, but also all the mystical character of his race." The peasant undressed, "mounted the model stand as if he had never posed; he

These studies of dancers are by Edgar Degas, who, like his friend Rodin, was intent on capturing movement in his art, and tried to analyze it with precision in drawings, paintings and sculptures. Degas, however, tended to freeze his models in the formal attitudes of dance—classical ballet *(above, top)* and flamenco *(above)*—which sometimes gave his work a static quality.

planted himself, head up, torso straight, at the same time supported by his two legs, opened like a compass. The movement was so right, so determined and so true that I cried, 'But it's a walking man!' I immediately resolved to make what I had seen." At the same time, Rodin asserted, he thought of a possible John the Baptist.

Evidently, the peasant only very distantly suggested a saint—Rodin wrote that he was "a dreadful creature," with a laugh like a wolf's. But he strode and stretched magnificently. It was this, not some faint religious reference, that seized Rodin. *St. John* needs no title: its true expressiveness lies in the body's movement.

But if both *St. John* and *The Walking Man* are principally displaying motion, it is motion of an extraordinary kind. A first sight of the two figures is oddly disconcerting: this is not the way a man actually walks. In each of the Rodin figures the feet are firmly planted even as the body swings ahead—manifestly a physical impossibility, yet a deliberate decision by Rodin. As he explained it, he sought to "display simultaneously . . . views of an object which in fact can be seen only successively." Thus *The Walking Man* and *St. John* reflect not just an instant of motion but a process, a sequence, one might say a scenario, from the beginning of the stride to its conclusion.

Rodin saw a great difference between sculpture and photography in the way they captured motion. A photographed subject was seen "suddenly stricken with paralysis and petrified in his pose . . . fixed in mid-air," and in this instantaneous record "there is no progressive development as there is in art. . . . It is the artist who is truthful and it is the photographer who lies, for in reality time does not stop, and if the artist succeeds in producing the impression of a movement that takes several moments for accomplishment, his work is much less *(ar-tificial)* than the scientific image, in which time is abruptly suspended."

It might be argued that Rodin's thesis was reinforced by the advent of the motion-picture camera. Each of the frames taken on a roll of movie film stops the action of the moment; when the individual pictures are rapidly projected in the appropriate sequence the human eye sees motion, not a series of halted actions. Rodin was saying, in effect, that forms are not fixed, but are always in a state of changing into others; being is a part of becoming, and it is a function of art to find coherent meaning in that flux. In this belief there was an affinity between Rodin and the contemporary Impressionist painters, who were intent on evoking the play of sunlight and air on trees, water and the open landscape. To the Impressionists the dimension of time was as important an element of art as it was to Rodin. In particular, in his view of the importance of seeing a form through a sequence of movements, Rodin was akin to Edgar Degas, who in his ballet paintings and sculptures was presenting much the same idea.

Rodin's preoccupation with movement was complicated by his habit of sculpturing fragments. To some critics these forms were simply "incomplete," accidents more than creative designs. A story, probably maliciously apocryphal, has it that on his return to Paris Rodin found that some casts shipped from Brussels had lost head or limbs in transit, a common occurrence then. Casts were picked up in their crates by local draymen, thrown amid ordinary railroad freight and delivered by more draymen; thus they were frequently shattered, especially when the weather was cold. Rodin, the story goes, restored some, but found others to his liking as they were and decided not to bother with them. Whatever the worth of this tale, it is known that on Rodin's Italian trip he had been as much drawn to Roman fragmentary remains as to Michelangelo's unfinished marbles.

Years later, when challenged about the headlessness of *The Walking Man*, he replied, "A head is superfluous for walking." Although his incomplete figures were termed "playthings of his imagination," they were actually far more. What he sought was the essential that survived the batterings of time. A meaningful part might be just as suggestive of life as the whole—indeed, its embodiment or microcosm or symbol. Whether one "finished" a work in the conventional sense did not matter: a rough detail of trunk or hand or foot or brow might convey the whole. And what, really, was meant by "finished"? "Are the cathedrals finished?" Rodin once snapped.

Rodin came to believe that a fragment should be considered an autonomous work. In so doing, he divorced sculpture from the idea of the formal likeness and heralded the day when artists began to insist that form had a life of its own. But in 1878 he appears not to have seen *The Walking Man* for the revolutionary work that it was. Or perhaps he did not wish to use it to challenge public taste after his bruising experience with *The Age of Bronze*. In any event he kept it in his studio and did not show it in public until 1900, although many artists, friends and students became familiar with it long before then. The writer Anatole France, pondering the battered shape of *The Walking Man* and other Rodin works, commented that the sculptor "collaborated too much with catastrophe." But Rodin did submit the *St. John* to the Salon of 1880 complete with head and arms (and a fig leaf too; Salon jurors could be sticky on such points).

Considering its size—the figure stands six feet six and three-quarter inches tall and is therefore much taller than the average 19th Century Frenchman—Rodin hoped that no one could revive *The Age of Bronze* canard and accuse him of having cast the work from the living body. The hope was vain; one critic snidely suggested that "he must have had a large man for his model." The sheer dramatic power of *St. John* overwhelmed many of the critics. There were those who found it ugly and vulgarly posed, or objected to the placement of the feet. But one newspaper commentator called the statue "a marvel of reality," noting: "*St. John* comes toward you with long steps, mouth open, hand raised. What fire in his looks and on his lips! What authority in his gesture!" The Salon jurors, while less rhapsodic, saw merit in the work, too; *St. John* carried off a prize—a third in the sculpture category.

Whether one approved of his work or not, Rodin was now a presence to be taken seriously. There was talk in art circles about him; there were students who came in groups to his studio to meet him and see more of what he was doing, to tell him they scorned the charges

Unlike Degas, Rodin preferred to catch his models in informal poses, as they walked about his studio, bent to retrieve some object, or, as shown above, engaged in limbering-up exercises, which obviously could not be sustained for long. As a result, these two figurines seem more buoyant, more capable of spontaneous, continuous movement, than the dancers depicted by Degas.

During his years as a designer at the Sèvres factory Rodin made the mother-and-child sketch above as a decorative motif for a porcelain vase. The effect of muscular vitality was much weakened in the version an anonymous craftsman made for the finished product *(below)*. Rodin later translated the same design into a freestanding sculpture entitled "*I am beautiful*" *(page 109)*.

about *The Age of Bronze.* To these aspiring artists, Rodin seemed worthy of being classed with the ancients, and with Donatello and Michelangelo. He received them cordially, and showed them a work in progress. One student recalled: "He talked about art with an intelligence entirely new to us, and the only reference he made to himself was this: 'I only think of outlines, to see that they are right and just.' We left him with the impression that we had seen . . . a genius, who was sure to be the most powerful demoralizer of what is called 'the sculpture of the School' that we ever had."

The same student recorded his amazement at finding evidences of "commercial" projects underway in the studio. Rodin had readily acknowledged them; they were intended, he explained, "to get my bread." Shortly before his recognition at the 1880 Salon, he had accepted a proposal from his old employer, Carrier-Belleuse, that promised to give him some measure of financial security. Carrier-Belleuse had become art director of the national porcelain factory at Sèvres, just outside Paris, and he offered his ex-assistant a part-time post as a designer. This was not only a handsome gesture of reconciliation after their estrangement in Brussels, but a lucrative and interesting assignment. For a retainer of 170 francs a month, plus a bonus of three francs an hour when actually at work at Sèvres, Rodin went to work designing the stylish vases and delicate table ornaments that made the factory renowned throughout Europe.

He enjoyed himself in the pleasant century-old Sèvres plant, which was more a colony of craftsmen than a conventional factory. The "manufactory" had been placed there in 1756 at the instigation of Madame de Pompadour, mistress of Louis XV. It lay in a sylvan setting beside the Seine at the edge of the royal park of Saint-Cloud, close to leafy avenues and cascades. Rodin—or at least that side of him always drawn to 18th Century taste—responded to the Sèvres scene by immersing himself in it. A fellow designer noted that he became so absorbed in his ornamental vases that he failed to hear the luncheon bell; after being reminded, he "very slowly detached his eyes from the object he was working on, as though reluctant to be awakened." At Sèvres, his friend the art critic Roger Marx noted, Rodin "forgot all rancor, dedicated himself without reservation, his mind at ease and full of joy." This was not the whole truth: there was always the other Rodin, the man grappling on off days with his powerful experiments in Paris. But his work in the light, elegant, traditional vein desired at Sèvres was so spirited as to strike critics as highly original in itself. Marx, an early admirer of Rodin's *St. John*, wrote of the unique "*frisson de volupté*"—the shudder of voluptuousness—that he imparted to his decorative pieces. Another critic rhapsodized in the *Journal des Artistes* about Rodin's *Vase of Pompeii*, a piece decorated with a fanciful frieze that showed figures making offerings to Ceres, goddess of agriculture and fertility, and to Bacchus, god of wine. "The caprices of M. Rodin's imagination," he wrote, "are as delicate as a breath borne on a gentle breeze. He is the living proof that a beautiful disorder is an effect of art. . . . Everywhere a strange variety, everywhere a delicious fancy. . . ."

A man so many-faceted was presumably an interesting one to meet. Hostesses and littérateurs began to seek out this personality with the bristling beard and the capacity to produce *frissons de volupté.* But at formal gatherings he had very little to say; the period of his loquaciousness lay in the future. One of his new friends was the popular writer Léon Cladel, who held large Sunday receptions for writers and artists at his villa in Sèvres; Rodin was given to long silences at them, and Cladel's young daughter Judith (one day to be Rodin's biographer) was struck by "the remarkable shyness that made the sculptor blush whenever he was addressed." Yet some attraction was making itself felt, for Rodin, while still living the life of a mere "art mason," or "workman," as he chose to describe his calling, was received into several influential Paris salons, those periodic gatherings at private homes where politics, art and literature were discussed. Rodin became a frequent guest of the brilliant and stylish Mme. Edmond Adam, founder of the literary journal *La Nouvelle Revue* and a poet and essayist of note.

The intellectual and political salon presided over by a vivacious woman of high social position was a traditional French institution, and it reached new heights of importance—or at least self-importance—in the great houses of the Faubourg Saint-Germain in the years of *la belle époque.* Often a salon was built around one male "lion" of distinction who, next to its hostess, was its chief attraction. Mme. Arman de Caillavet's was built around her lover, Anatole France; Mme. Adam's around Léon Gambetta, President of the Chamber of Deputies. Rodin was a very minor figure in a company at Mme. Adam's that included such luminaries as the composer Charles Gounod, whose opera *Faust* was currently a hit; the future Premier René Waldeck-Rousseau; and, on rare occasions, the great Victor Hugo. Rodin was invited initially because Gambetta—perhaps the most prestigious public figure in France —had expressed a wish to meet the creator of the controversial *Age of Bronze.* Mme. Adam located and invited Rodin, who for all his reticence was eager for recognition; Gambetta was much taken with him and spoke of him to several ministers.

It was probably Gambetta who brought Rodin to the attention of a particularly important official, Edmond Turquet, Undersecretary of the Ministry of Fine Arts and an admirer of *The Age of Bronze.* Earlier, Rodin had appealed to Turquet's office for vindication of his claims about the sculpture; Turquet ordered an investigation and supported them. Perhaps a word from Gambetta strengthened Turquet in his move to buy the work for the state and have it erected in the Luxembourg Gardens in 1880. Rodin and Turquet themselves met at about this time—introduced by Turquet's brother-in-law, a painter employed at Sèvres —and the relationship that now began became one of the most strategic and rewarding of Rodin's lifetime.

Turquet was by no means an art expert, but a political appointee entrusted with wide powers of art patronage. By profession he was a lawyer who had risen to become a magistrate and public prosecutor under the Second Empire and then an influential deputy under the Third Republic; by predilection he was an enthusiast for the new in art, particularly the work of Édouard Manet. Rodin once remarked that although Turquet knew no more about art than did other high-placed officials, he was extraordinarily fair-minded. The Undersecretary and the sculptor hit it off extremely well and became firm friends. The extent of Turquet's powers (which, among others, embraced ultimate control over appointments at Sèvres) was also not lost on Rodin.

Not long after they met, Turquet won for Rodin his first public commission of major importance—as it turned out, the most important of his entire career. It was a portal for a proposed museum of decorative arts in Paris, a pair of doors to be sculpted on a monumental scale. Eventually entitled *The Gates of Hell*, this enormous project was to absorb much of Rodin's energy for decades. In 1880, however, its immediate advantage was that it gave him what he perhaps desired most: an ample studio without cost, one Turquet assigned him in the Dépôt des Marbres in the Rue de l'Université on the Left Bank, where the government stored blocks of marble for distribution to favored sculptors and also provided working space for a few artists. Here, behind a courtyard littered with roughhewn stones and casts, was an official haven that provided some prestige, along with a sure supply of coal.

There, while brooding on the first figures for *The Gates*, Rodin found time to make several busts of friends, more with the thought of pleasure than of possible sales. He made an admiring head of Carrier-Belleuse, with whom he was now on the best of terms—a bust molded very much in 18th Century style, as befitted its portly, amiable subject. He sculpted his Petite École classmate and companion, the painter Alphonse Legros. The work makes Legros look grave and severe, but he liked it, reciprocating with an admiring oil portrait of Rodin exuding strength and pride. The sculptor Jules Dalou also sat for Rodin. He, too, had been a fellow student at the Petite École, and was perhaps Rodin's closest friend. Dalou was something of a radical in politics, if not in art, and had been appointed a director of the Louvre by the extremist Commune that briefly seized the government of Paris at the end of the Franco-Prussian War. Exiled by the Third Republic, he had returned home in 1879. The two men held an emotional reunion and Rodin sculpted Dalou showing him lean, somber, strained by time and experience *(page 83)*. (Dalou was not pleased by the realistic result.) Another Rodin sitter was the influential Henri de Rochefort, a sharp-tongued editor of the newspaper *L'Intransigeant*. (Rochefort did not like his bust either, and kept it in an attic.)

Rodin was also beginning to receive private commissions and to sell his works to individual patrons. Baroness Nathaniel de Rothschild of the banking dynasty set such sales in motion early in the 1880s when she bought a frivolous Rodin figure called *Girl Eavesdropping*. During the same period Rodin was introduced to a reigning lady of fashion, Madame Luisa Lynch de Morla Vicuña, the beautiful French wife of the Chilean Ambassador, and she helped launch him as a producer of portrait busts for the stylish. With the increased income from such commissions, Rodin was able to stop working at Sèvres.

By early 1881 he was earning enough money to undertake a trip to

England that advanced his fortunes further. He knew no English, had no English connections and went chiefly to visit Legros, who was teaching in London. Rodin had gotten off to an unhappy start with England some years before when he entered a competition for a London monument to Lord Byron; his entry was lost, for reasons never determined. But Legros was well established there and introduced Rodin to the poet and critic William Ernest Henley, editor of the *Magazine of Art*, who promptly took him in as a friend and also introduced him to another well-known man of letters, Robert Louis Stevenson.

Rodin's visit was a highly agreeable one. Henley, Stevenson and the poet Robert Browning were all drawn to him, and he found himself taken up in the sophisticated drawing rooms of Chelsea as he had been in the salons of the Faubourg Saint-Germain. In 1882, after his return home, his *St. John* was exhibited at the Royal Academy in London; a year later several of his works were being shown there, and he was back for another visit, entranced by the atmosphere of the city, the spires and bridges of Westminster. In a country with no great sculptor of its own Rodin was the subject of considerable attention. In 1884 *The Age of Bronze* was accepted by the Academy as a guest exhibit, and there was keen interest in it, especially among those who knew of its earlier difficulties in Brussels and Paris. Henley proclaimed it original and distinctive, and Rodin's other literary friends were equally admiring.

He was not, however, an unqualified success in London. In 1886 *The Times* carried a blast at his work by a Royal Academician who noted the radical Frenchman's inability to win prizes in his own country. Stevenson took up arms in *The Times:* "The public are weary of statues that say nothing. Well, here is a man coming forward, whose statues live and speak, and speak things worth uttering. Give him time, spare him nicknames and the cant of cliques, and I venture to predict . . . he will take a place in the public heart."

Moved, Rodin gratefully sent Stevenson a small plaster cast of his new amorous pair, *Eternal Springtime (page 110)*. The cast accompanied Stevenson, who suffered from tuberculosis, when he left England in 1887 and settled in Samoa in hopes of a cure. Henley, for his part, received a copy of *The Man with the Broken Nose* from Rodin in gratitude for his support. Henley responded, writing of the head, "It remains eternally beautiful. . . . You have not lacked disappointments, my friend; on the contrary, I know that you have struggled hard, suffered much. . . . You work for the centuries to come."

Rodin enjoyed all his male associations at home and abroad, but in these middle years women were his chief interest, personally and artistically. His sculptures grew increasingly erotic, showing couples united in every stage of passion. Yet this was sensual portraiture with a difference—neither frivolous nor naughty, as was Boucher's titillating painting of a bare-bottomed royal mistress or Bouguereau's prizewinning canvas of a whole flight of nymphs similarly displayed.

The couples sculpted by Rodin are not just playing games; the women in these works are not toys but full participating partners. Males and females are drawn together by a mutual urge for fulfillment; yet

Robert Louis Stevenson posed for this picture a few years before he settled in Samoa. When he left England he took with him a gift from Rodin, the small erotic sculpture *Eternal Springtime (page 110)*. The author and the artist shared a temperamental affinity: each had a markedly sensual nature. Stevenson's was kept in check by his Scottish Calvinist background, but he applauded Rodin's frank sculptural treatment of love and advocated an unhypocritical approach to the display of physical passion in art.

amid this sweep of desire there are currents of questioning and gestures of restraint. As a result, the sculptures display a subtle psychological balance. In *Eternal Springtime* the girl is evidently torn between the impulse to give herself and to withhold—at least for a while. In *Fugit Amor (page 103)* a girl glides like a fish from beneath her lover's hold. In *The Kiss* there is again an intimate balance of impulses—although little doubt exists that consummation will soon be reached. Rodin's approach to these sculptures, he said, was one of homage to woman and her body—no longer merely submitting to man, but matching him in ardor. Rodin aimed to express that ardor without artifice. One critic who saw what he meant by such forthrightness called him "the Homer of woman's body."

In Rodin's private life his admiration for women soon led straight to the bed. Models, students, servants, seamstresses and society sitters alike attracted him. The ladies' identities, with a few exceptions, remain publicly unknown, but Rose knew them, and one day a physician whom Rodin summoned to her bedside when she was ill found her delirious, "calling invectives on the mistresses of Rodin." But she could not leave him. On one memorable occasion she burst into his studio in a suspicious fury. Rodin cautiously emerged from behind a partition. She surged toward it, but Rodin outmaneuvered her. As they circled, Rodin keeping between her and the partition, he picked up a piece of clay and began modeling her infuriated face. When she calmed down, Rodin presented her with a finished mask: "Thank you, my dear . . . this is to let you see how beautiful you are when you're angry." The studio assistant who witnessed the encounter wrote that "there was nothing she could do with that man," but discreetly did not mention who was behind the partition.

Rodin's reputation as a redoubtable sexual performer was established. Living with Rose in a dark and gloomy house he bought in the 1880s in the Rue des Grands-Augustins near the Seine, he stole away from her to assignations in an astonishing number of studios and retreats. A sign posted on the door of his studio at the Dépôt des Marbres sometimes told visitors: "M. Rodin is absent, visiting cathedrals." The "cathedral" more likely was a medieval tower at Nemours where he had one of his hideaways.

Amid such passing diversions, Camille Claudel entered his life. Twenty years his junior, she held him for years in an embrace different from any he had known before. Their relationship was stormy, tortuous, often explosive and doomed to end bitterly, but she was the great love of his life—although he could not forsake the home comforts of Rose any more than Rose could leave him. Camille, far from being just another alluring bedmate, was a young woman of high pride, spirit, status, independence and talent. Born of a solid bourgeois family, she had proved herself a gifted student of art, and it was as an aspiring sculptor that she met Rodin, who had been asked to advise a class she belonged to. She was also, in the parlance of the day, a "new woman"—a rebel against parental authority and restriction and so self-liberated that she set up her own studio on the Left Bank before she was 20. Moreover, she was hauntingly beautiful. One writer spoke of her "magnificent eyes, pale green, suggesting forest shoots." (She apparently so bemused the admirers who wrote of her that it is not clear to this day whether her eyes were blue, green or gray; they were evidently of the shade that changes with the light and with the eye of the observer.) Her brother Paul Claudel, later famous as a poet and statesman, wrote of her "perfect brow . . . a generous mouth, proud rather than sensual . . . a vivid air of courage, of candor, of superiority, of gaiety."

A photograph of Camille in her twenties gives an impression of smoldering intensity guarded by loftiness and strength. Rodin was overwhelmed by her, and she by him: they became not only lovers but profound partners in experience. It was after he met her that his sculptures took on their extraordinary erotic power. Here, alive, was the superior female he had been dreaming of in art. Camille posed for him, in turn sculpted him, and collaborated with him in his studio. Her skill was remarkable: she had studied anatomy on her own, dissected animals, knew the pull and strain of muscles almost as well as Rodin did and in fact contributed many a hand or limb to the figures on which he was working. Visitors saw the lovers laboring side by side in the Dépôt des Marbres, smocks flecked with clay. While seated beside him she inspired one of his most startling sculptures—a shape in which her head appears, ineffably delicate and reflective, rising out of a roughhewn square block of stone. He called the work *Thought* perhaps as a counterpart to his masculine *The Thinker*; actually, like Botticelli's *Venus*, it suggests beauty emerging from primordial nature.

When Camille sculpted Rodin, it was in a style akin to his own rough, realistic manner with men. After Rodin had her head of him shown at an exhibition of his own works, there were critics who suggested that he was simply doing a favor for a very favored pupil. Rodin answered gallantly but accurately: "I helped her find gold in art, but it was all in herself." The critic Octave Mirbeau, studying some of Camille's other work, wrote that she was "a woman of genius." The sculptor Aristide Maillol in time proclaimed her a major French artist in her own right.

Although Rodin and Camille worked and slept together, they did not openly live together. They sequestered themselves in one or another of his retreats and on occasion traveled together, once for several months. Always, in Rodin's double life, there was Rose, the caretaker to whom he regularly returned. On several occasions the rival women met, and there are stories of fishwife screeching and even hair-pulling when they did. Rodin tried to assuage Rose: at one point during an absence from Paris and the Rue des Grands-Augustins house he wrote: "I think of how much you must have loved me to put up with my caprices . . . I remain, in all tenderness, your Rodin."

Camille, ardent mistress and accomplished artist, was far from being a caprice: she and Rodin carried on their stormy affair for 15 turbulent years. These were also the years of his most formidable and original works—*The Burghers of Calais*, an utterly unconventional monument for a provincial city, and *The Gates of Hell*, his unfulfilled masterpiece.

Rodin's longtime mistress Camille Claudel wears a somber look in the photograph above, suggesting her serious outlook on life, but in her art she was often capable of humor. Although the bust she executed of Rodin *(below)* makes him appear ruggedly handsome —which may be why it was his favorite portrait of himself—Camille also engraved a dry-point profile of her lover that depicts him as a Teddy-bear type with a bulbous nose.

A Reluctant Rebel

From the beginning, Rodin found himself at odds with the Parisian art establishment. He had not set out to spark a rebellion; schooled traditionally, he yearned for academic success. But his work almost always raised a storm of controversy. The first sculpture he submitted to the Salon, in 1864 *(right)*, was summarily rejected. Possibly the Salon jury was irate because Rodin had submitted only a fragmentary face; the back of the clay head had fallen off in an accident. More likely, it was the raw realism of the work that shocked the staid judges.

For the next decade and a half, Rodin worked at his art while compelled to earn a living at mundane jobs —fashioning bric-a-brac and ornamental statuary—in Paris and Brussels. After a brief trip to Italy, where he studied Donatello and Michelangelo, he returned to Paris more convinced than ever that "nature tells the whole story." The maxim was hardly revolutionary, yet Rodin's first full-scale work, *The Age of Bronze,* was heaped with abuse after its initial exhibition in 1877. To those who admired Neoclassicism, Rodin's style was a gross affront. They believed that sculpture should show handsome men and beautiful women idealized to cool perfection. Rodin's figures looked real and ordinary, with bulging muscles and rough complexions. This fundamental difference in approach forced Rodin to battle the existing powers most of his life. But he never considered himself an iconoclast; his mission, he felt, was to restore vitality to sculpture.

Battered by age and work, the face of this old man was caught with poignant realism by Rodin. His first major portrait, it became a stylistic model for much of his later sculpture. Characteristically, it emphasizes such essentials as the texture of the skin, the structure of the skull and the psychological state of the subject himself. More than most sculptors of his time, Rodin believed that an individual's personality was directly revealed by his physical features.

The Man with the Broken Nose, 1864
RODIN MUSEUM, PARIS

The Age of Bronze is an exquisitely worked figure of a well-proportioned young man, his attitude slightly dreamy, his pose a trifle puzzling. But to those who viewed the original plaster version at the Salon of 1877, the figure was rank heresy. The sculpture was so lifelike that it was immediately assumed to have been cast directly from a living man. Almost as shocking was its lack of a clear theme. The taste of the time demanded that a statue symbolize some noble human act drawn from history or mythology. As one critic put it, Rodin's work was only "an astonishingly exact copy of a low type."

In a way, Rodin had asked for such taunts. Some time earlier he had entitled the figure *The Vanquished* and placed a spear in the left hand, a prop that would have suggested a theme. But he removed the spear because it blocked the view of the torso from certain angles. Rodin tried to indicate the theme by the final title he gave the work, *The Age of Bronze*, denoting that prehistoric time when man, strengthened by his newly developed metal tools and weapons, began to emerge from the primitive world of the cave. Still, few understood Rodin's subtle reference.

The sculpture owes much to Michelangelo's *Dying Slave*, which Rodin had studied at the Louvre; he also had the Italian master in mind after his recent tour of Italy. As he worked on the figure, he tried to emulate Michelangelo's mastery of the human body, yet remain true to his own view of nature. He scrambled up ladders to observe his model from all angles and even made clay sketches for the purpose of studying them by the flicker of candlelight. As a result, the figure is alive with the interaction of highlights and shadows. Yet for all his effort Rodin's work was again dismissed by critics. He won over one important admirer, however, Edmond Turquet, an art lover and government minister, who later convinced the French state to buy the work.

The Age of Bronze, 1876-1877

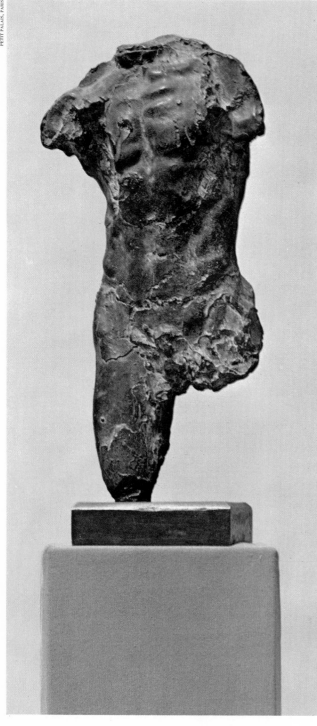

Torso (study for *The Walking Man*), 1877-1878

The Walking Man, 1877-1878

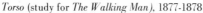

A desire to win approval from the Salon public led Rodin to create one of his finest naturalistic works, *St. John the Baptist Preaching (opposite)*. It began as an abstracted torso, the chest cleft and gashed *(above)*. Rodin then set the torso on well-muscled legs and called it *The Walking Man (above, right)*. But by now he had learned that such fragmented works were too unorthodox for wide acceptance. Before the Salon of 1880 he added a head, arms and the mandatory fig leaf. Thus enhanced, *St. John* won a third prize.

"The sculptor compels . . . the spectator to follow the development of an act in an individual," Rodin once said, noting that in this way the artist generates "the illusion of beholding the movement performed." *St. John* illustrates this concept perfectly. Although both feet are placed solidly on the ground, the figure pulses with vitality and motion. How the effect of walking is achieved can be seen by letting one's eye move up the back leg, across the hips and down the front leg. Although no shift of weight takes place, it *seems* to, and the illusion of movement is created. This remarkable technical triumph was lost on many critics. Again, however, the admiring Minister Turquet encouraged the government to buy the work, and Rodin was on his way to fame.

St. John the Baptist Preaching, 1878

It was through his portraits that Rodin finally won popular acceptance and financial independence. He started by portraying such intimates as his lifelong companion Rose Beuret, his fellow sculptor Jules Dalou, his mistress Camille Claudel and Mrs. John Russell, an Italian-born beauty whom Rodin sculpted often. His genius for portraying personality eventually attracted the patronage of the wealthy and famous, but not all his sitters agreed with his views of them. Georges Clemenceau, later to be Premier of France, insisted that his portrait be exhibited as *Bust of an Unknown*. The playwright George Bernard Shaw had a more typical reaction: he respected Rodin greatly despite unsuspected hazards during his sittings. As Rodin sculpted, he would spray water from his mouth to keep the clay moist and workable. But, as Shaw later wrote, "absorbed in his work, he did not always aim well and soaked my clothes."

So keen was Rodin's perception of his subjects that he could work even in their absence. To finish his portrait of composer Gustav Mahler—who had left Paris—Rodin used his own secretary, a man who resembled the musician, as the model. The finished work was not only a good likeness of Mahler but a remarkable reflection of his personality.

Mignon (Rose Beuret), bronze, 18

Mrs. John Russell, silver, before 1888

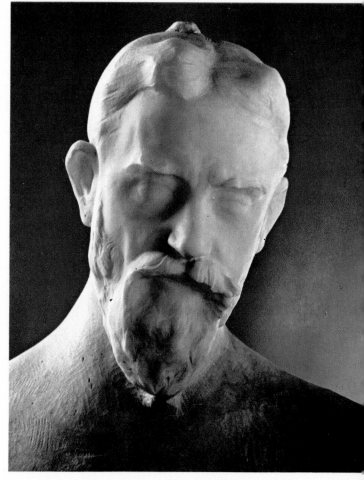

George Bernard Shaw, marble, 19

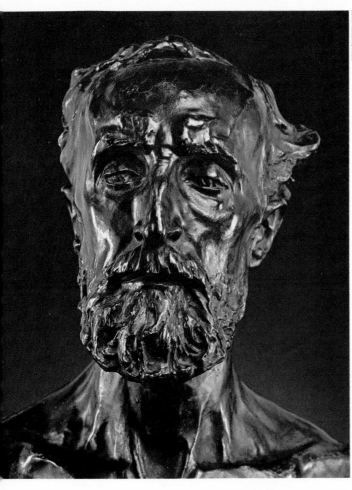

Jules Dalou, bronze, 1883

Camille Claudel, bronze, 1884

Gustav Mahler, bronze, 1909

Georges Clemenceau, bronze, 1911

IV

Into the Inferno

Western literature and art have produced three great conceptions of hell: that of the poet Dante in his *Inferno*, that of Michelangelo in his fresco *The Last Judgment* on the altar wall of the Sistine Chapel and that of Rodin in his *Gates of Hell (pages 96-111)*.

Rodin's sculpture is a work monumental in every way. As finally cast in bronze, it stands 21 feet high, 13 feet wide and about 3 feet deep. It is peopled with some 180 agonized figures in every conceivable posture. It contains themes not only from Dante's *Inferno*, but from the Bible, from medieval accounts of hell and damnation, from contemporary French poetry—specifically, Baudelaire's despairing *Flowers of Evil*—and from Rodin's own fertile imagination. Nothing remotely like it had been seen up to then in the world of sculpture, or has been seen since.

Rodin worked on this gargantuan opus, on and off, for 37 years, beginning in 1880. It started as a commission from the French government for an ornamental portal for a projected Paris museum of decorative arts. The task was viable enough: to provide an inviting entrance to a show place of such objects as Gobelin tapestries, Sèvres porcelain, ormolu tabletops, fancy clocks and figurines. But Rodin's friend Turquet, through whom he received the commission, evidently lacked any clear idea of what he was looking for. All the Undersecretary of the Ministry of Fine Arts seems to have known was that he wanted a large pair of doors and that he wanted Rodin to execute them. As for the theme, Turquet was perfectly willing to let Rodin choose it himself. Of all possible subjects, few could have been less in keeping with a repository of the lighter arts than the one Rodin did choose—that of lost spirits doomed to eternal perdition. In fact, such was the gulf between Rodin's concept of the commission and its stated purpose that at one point he reportedly even considered placing on the cornice of his doors the inscription Dante saw on the gates at the entrance to his Inferno: "Abandon hope, all ye who enter here."

For the better part of a decade Rodin concentrated his energies on *The Gates*, designing and redesigning them, and despite other subsequent

Arms raised in despair, this nude typifies the themes of agony and frustration that Rodin dealt with in his epic *Gates of Hell*. A master of expressive posture and gesture, Rodin created attitudes like this and used them in various ways on the portal and in separate sculptures. This figure is seen twice on *The Gates*, clutching at a writhing woman *(pages 102 and 106)*. He also appears back to back with the female figure in *Fugit Amor (page 103)*.

The Prodigal, bronze, 1886

Rodin posed with friends and white-smocked assistants in his Meudon studio before the still-unfinished full-scale plaster model of *The Gates of Hell*. Standing at the artist's right is Léonce Bénédite, Rodin's choice as the first curator of the collection of works he had recently given to the French state. (Bénédite has casually hung his hat on a corner of the model.) In the foreground is Eugène Rudier, son of the director of the foundry where Rodin's bronzes were cast. It was the Rudier foundry that finally, about 1928, produced two bronze casts of *The Gates*, an undertaking financed by the American Jules Mastbaum, who built his fortune on a chain of movie theaters. Mastbaum's generosity not only made it possible for his native city of Philadelphia to boast its own Rodin Museum —where one of the casts of *The Gates* stands —but also restored Rodin's run-down studio at Meudon after the sculptor's death.

preoccupations he returned to them again and again until his death in 1917, adding figures here, subtracting others there. In relation to his herculean effort the financial reward was minimal. Beginning with an 8,000-franc fee, the government grants provided him finally totaled 30,000 francs—this for a man who was later to command 40,000 francs for a single portrait bust.

Moreover, the museum of decorative arts was never built. Its construction was to have been financed by a public lottery that was never held. Thus, even as the state made periodic grants to Rodin to pursue *The Gates*, the prospect of a place for them dimmed, and although Rodin plunged ahead, any idea of their possible usefulness faded. Rodin's huge plaster casts in the government-owned Dépôt des Marbres, in which he continued to enjoy free working space, became a kind of mammoth tableau, experimental and ever-changing. The work he had planned as a functioning entryway turned into a mere studio exercise. *The Gates* were not even cast in bronze until almost a decade after Rodin's death, and then only because of the generosity of a wealthy

American admirer, Jules Mastbaum. The prime cast now adorns the front of the Rodin Museum in Philadelphia; the three other casts are in Paris, Zurich and Tokyo. Not one of them actually serves as a pair of doors; they do not open, they lead nowhere. In this sense *The Gates* were a colossal failure.

At the same time, *The Gates* represent the most ambitious undertaking of Rodin's lifetime, and his most remarkable. They became in effect a world of his own making, a panorama of all his ideas and imaginings, and the source of many of his other major works. *The Kiss, The Thinker, The Prodigal, Fugit Amor* and *Eternal Springtime* were all outgrowths of *The Gates*, and all of them were later expanded into separate sculptures; *The Thinker*, for one, was designed to be placed in the center of the tympanum of *The Gates*, but was subsequently enlarged three times into an individual work, six feet seven inches high.

Had Rodin foreseen the complications that lay ahead, he might never have undertaken *The Gates*. But as it was, the news that a monumental portal was under consideration enormously excited him. From every standpoint it seemed a rare challenge for a sculptor, and certain to win him considerable fame. Rodin made no bones about his eagerness for the assignment. When he literally importuned Turquet for the job, his friend reacted with bureaucratic caution. He explained that he did not wish to lay himself open to charges of favoritism, but that if a few artists —Carrier-Belleuse, for instance—were to recommend Rodin he would be unable to refuse. Taking the hint, Rodin rounded up the same colleagues who had come to his defense over the integrity of *The Age of Bronze*. They petitioned the Ministry of Fine Arts on his behalf—and the commission was his.

So far as is known, the only clue Rodin gave Turquet of his working plan for *The Gates* was to tell him: "I'll make a lot of small-sized figures, so that people won't accuse me again of casting from living models." In this obvious reference to the charges leveled at him several years earlier about *The Age of Bronze* Rodin revealed that he was still smarting over the affair, and still seeking vindication. Years later he was to repeat that his intent with *The Gates* had been to prove that he did not cast from life, so that "the lies thrown at me could not be repeated," although he added that he had been out simply for "color and effect," without any "method or subject, scheme of illustration . . . or intended moral purpose."

Obviously, however, he had more than vindication or color and effect in mind. As it happened, in the period just before the commissioning of *The Gates*, Rodin, always an avid reader, had been immersing himself in Dante's *Inferno*. Like most readers he was fascinated by the account of Dante's descent into the bowels of the earth, guided by the ancient Roman poet Vergil, in search of the Kingdom of God, and of their traversing the nine concentric layers of hell, viewing the sufferings inflicted on the damned, pausing in horror to let those doomed for eternity recount the reasons for their punishment. "I lived a year with Dante," Rodin remembered, "drawing the . . . circles of his hell." He admired Dante, as he did Michelangelo, for the poignancy of his expression of ordeal and suffering, for his recognition of man's essentially tragic fate, and for the grandeur of his conceptions; in Rodin's view the rings of Dante's hell constituted a cosmology comparable to that of Michelangelo's Sistine ceiling and *Last Judgment*. Moreover, Rodin saw Dante as a kind of sculptor—as he put it, "a literary sculptor: he speaks in gestures as well as in words." As Judith Cladel noted in her biography of Rodin, he appears to have felt himself in "secret rapport" with the poet, just as with Michelangelo.

Well before there was any talk of Turquet's portal, Rodin had drawn, for his own interest, sheaves of figures based on his reading of the *Inferno:* couples locked in ardent but fatal embrace, sinners pursued by serpents, Dante and Vergil recoiling before the spectacle of hell's agony and retribution. Like other 19th Century artists, Rodin was particularly haunted by the specter of Ugolino, the once-proud Count of Pisa who, in the 13th Century, was condemned for betraying his city, imprisoned with his young sons and forced to watch them die of starvation. In Dante's version, Ugolino then starves to death himself; the grisly version of this tale favored in the 19th Century, however, was that Ugolino devoured his sons after they died. Rodin's studies of this grim subject begin with tortuous but tender sketches of Ugolino cradling his dying sons and go on to depict the bestialized father pouncing upon their flesh. In effect, the sketches are progressive portrayals of human dissolution and degradation. In due course, a sculpted version of Ugolino writhing above his sons came about, to be placed upon *The Gates*—one of those "small figures" Rodin promised Turquet, small in size, but large in horror *(pages 100 and 101)*.

Dante, however, served only as a "starting point," as Rodin himself explained. Much as the poet's spirit broods over *The Gates*, relatively little of the specific content of the *Inferno* appears among the figures Rodin produced. In addition to Ugolino, there are recurring images of Paolo Malatesta and his sister-in-law Francesca da Rimini, the tragic 13th Century lovers doomed to pay for their illicit passion in a torment of eternal but unrealized desire. Atop the cornice is a trio of grieving male nudes called *The Three Shades*, their arms pointing to the chaos below. Although they are not mentioned in Dante, they may have been intended to represent the despairing inscription he saw over the entrance to his hell. In time, as Rodin's own creative imagination took fire, numbers of Biblical and mythological characters emerged from his hand—a suppliant *Prodigal*, a massive *Adam*, a swelling maternal *Eve*, an array of Sirens, symbols of passion and desire. In addition, he executed many figures that are entirely unidentifiable, anonymous sufferers so torn and fragmented in form that it is not possible to say whether they are male or female, sinful man or primeval blob. There is a frieze Rodin called *Heads of the Damned* that resembles a cabinet of battered relics. Some of the heads are faceless, one has the face of Rodin's *St. John the Baptist*, and one is a likeness—of all people—of the sculptor's beloved Camille Claudel, who in these years was often at his side posing for or assisting in the sculpting of his figures. In the central place in the tympanum there appears to be a seat. It is occupied not by

Christ—as in medieval representations of the Last Judgment—but by *The Thinker*, in tortured reverie above all the turmoil. Rodin had abandoned Dante's cosmology and substituted his own, its focus not on damnation but on human suffering.

The Ministry of Fine Arts had virtually no clues as to what was going on behind the closed doors of Rodin's studio. The project was underway only a few months when he wrote Turquet that he would need more than the time he had been allotted to complete the work, as well as an additional grant of 10,000 francs. By way of explanation he reported that he wished to create "two colossal figures" for either side of the portal—the figures that later turned out to be *Adam* and *Eve*. This was about all Rodin revealed of his plan; he did not even bother to send the Ministry any sketches. Despite official curiosity and concern, more money was granted Rodin late in 1881. After another year, still with no visible signs of progress from Rodin, he asked for more funds. At length, in January 1883, the Ministry decided that the time had come to check on the project.

Since Turquet himself did not wish to intrude on his friend, especially since he had not been asked to the studio, he sent an inspector named Roger Ballu to look in on the Dépôt des Marbres. The resulting encounter was an odd one. Ballu presented himself at Rodin's door and was admitted to a great barn of a studio crowded with clay forms under moist wraps. But he was allowed to view just some of the works; Rodin himself carefully lifted the cloths. Fortunately Ballu was more than a policeman of truant art objects; he was a man of discernment. Although he found some of the figures strange, he was drawn to them and to Rodin as well. His report to Turquet was a model of judiciousness, and written with a flair not normally associated with the prose of bureaucrats. Ballu duly noted that he had not been able to see all the figures properly arranged in place but added: "M. Rodin's work is extremely interesting. This young sculptor reveals a really astonishing originality and power of expression, with overtones of anguish. Beneath the energy of the attitudes, beneath the vehemence of the poses expressive of movement, he conceals his disdain for, or rather his indifference to, a coldly sculptural style." The inspector was inclined to think that Rodin's work merited praise and encouragement. Before the end of the year he was back for another look. "The design of the work will, I think, be a startling one," he notified Turquet.

The emerging design for *The Gates* was indeed startling; it was, in fact, unprecedented. The obvious example for Rodin to have followed was Lorenzo Ghiberti's celebrated *Gates of Paradise* on the Baptistery in Florence. Fashioned in the 15th Century, these paired bronze doors, each with five panels depicting subjects from the Old Testament in exquisite relief, offered a scheme that might well have been adapted to Rodin's *Gates*. Rodin is known to have admired Ghiberti's work, and his first sketches show a desire to emulate the Florentine's plan, but he soon drew away from it, as he had from too close a relationship to Dante's *Inferno*.

Instead he tapped another source of inspiration: the portals of me-

One source of Rodin's inspiration for the overall design of his *Gates of Hell* was Lorenzo Ghiberti's gilt bronze portal on the east front of the Baptistery of the Cathedral of Florence, on which 10 panels of sculptured reliefs depict stories from the Old Testament. The splendor of Ghiberti's doors, executed between 1425 and 1452, moved his fellow Florentine Michelangelo to acclaim them as the "Gates of Paradise," the name by which they are still familiarly known. Some 50 years after Ghiberti finished his masterpiece, the lintel above it was adorned with three stone sculptures by Andrea Sansovino —representing St. John baptizing Christ while an angel looks on. Rodin's recollection of the striking effect of this trio of figures may have influenced the placement of the group called *The Three Shades (page 95)* above his *Gates.*

As Rodin developed his plan for *The Gates of Hell,* he made one very rough sketch in clay *(top)* and several watercolor drawings of the basic structural scheme. At this stage he was still very much under Ghiberti's influence. As Léonce Bénédite noted, the plan "conformed absolutely in its symmetrical arrangement to the Baptistery model." But gradually Rodin revised his concept. In the drawing above, the dark shadow at top center indicates that he was considering creating figures that stood forth prominently from the surface. Finally, Rodin decided on a tumultuous cascade of figures, in dramatic high relief and asymmetrically arranged—a far remove from the ordered composition and low relief of Ghiberti's doors.

dieval cathedrals. Rodin had seen a number of these magnificent doorways on his travels and had long been fascinated by their dramatic carvings of serried saints, kings, petitioners and the damned, some subdued in low relief, others jutting forth in high relief, still others standing in the round. Rodin well knew that the play of light on these contrasting surfaces generated the sense of movement he had been seeking all his artistic life. The more his own scheme developed, the more there was in it of the dynamism of the Gothic and Romanesque styles and less of the serenity of Ghiberti.

Nameless masters of still earlier eras also contributed to Rodin's grand design for *The Gates.* The medallions of heads, and the thick embrasures and beams, recall both the stark early-Christian doors of the Fifth Century basilica of St. Sabina in Rome and the portals of the Second Century Roman Pantheon, with their massive posts and overhanging lintels. Simultaneously, Rodin's scheme assimilated the influence of 17th Century baroque style, with its urge to break out from rigid frameworks and its love of swirling shapes in irrepressible movement. In *The Gates* figures leap forth from niches and apertures, some clambering over the structure, others falling from it headfirst, all in a riot of struggle and confusion. All this frenzied, chaotic activity takes place on a torn, savage, lavalike landscape pitted with holes and caves. Into these some forms crawl with just their legs and buttocks showing, while others are twisted into toadlike positions, diabolically grimacing. Figures that resemble High Renaissance cherubs tumble next to others that suggest medieval gargoyles. *The Prodigal,* naked and elongated, reaches out and agonizes, while nearby a withered harridan sinks down. No figure seems related to or interested in the next; there is no camaraderie in Rodin's hell.

There is, however, deliberate composition in the chaos. Stretching forms adjoin compressed forms, and figures emerging from the structure are juxtaposed with those disappearing into it, in an unending counterpoint that emphasizes the isolation of human beings in a mad world. Rodin recalled: "I followed my own imagination, my own sense of arrangement, movement, composition." His imagination was at fever pitch, and to the extent that his composition was intended to convey man's disarray, it succeeded. In effect, *The Gates* show us the hell within, the torment experienced by every man who suffers the assaults of fortune, who fights back, who glimpses beauty and reward, and who in the end is isolated and overcome. Perhaps the most characteristic figure of *The Gates* is *The Prodigal (page 84),* who reaches out helplessly, "his cries lost in the heavens," as Rodin described it, and whose gasping face is the embodiment of anguish over all that has been wasted and seems irretrievable.

Why should Rodin, outwardly so exuberant in his life and work as he entered his forties, have reflected such bleak conceptions in his great undertaking? Like most men, he was a mixture, sometimes somber, sometimes lighthearted, perhaps weighted a bit more than most to the serious side. But there is nothing in his personal life that suggests an immediate cause for the profound pessimism that seems to mark

The Gates. True, his existence with Rose was growing ever more stormy, and their son was little short of a disaster. But Rodin had suffered no searing tragedy since his sister's death 20 years earlier. His days and most of his nights were warmed by the companionship of Camille. Although he was not making much money, and there were still many rejections of his work, he was becoming increasingly well known, and his friends and supporters were multiplying.

It is possible to argue that Rodin saw *The Gates* merely as an opportunity to achieve something grandiose; that a theme suggested itself out of his reading and study; that his artistic imagination asserted itself —and that a concept came into being. But such an argument would be simplistic. *The Gates* are basically about rebels and outcasts, about persons who collided with society. Rodin's own relationship with the constituted order of his time was ambiguous from the start. He had set out to get himself accepted by the Establishment, to rise in it, to win prizes and awards. At the same time he was imbued with a sense of being outside it, fated to struggle alone, subject to extraordinary buffetings. From early years he had derived a certain pride from being an outsider, the man who would not conform. There is no doubt that he was closer in spirit to those who had suffered at society's hands than to those who had succeeded in it, as witness his first major works, *The Man with the Broken Nose*, that allegory of endurance, and also his *St. John the Baptist*, the solitary prophet of the rebirth of mankind—who was put to death.

Misfortune and rejection drew forth Rodin's deepest response, and it may well be that as his own chances of worldly success grew, he felt some compulsion—amid the temptations of conformity—to testify to this. He was aware of the troubles that await the individual who defies society, and intensely sympathetic; significantly, he chose to represent Adam and Eve—humanity's first rebels against a constituted order—as heroic figures. So *The Gates*, although harsh and brutal in their rendering, are actually compassionate in their intention. The forms heave and writhe in contorted and pitiable positions because they are all too human; they suffer as mankind suffers, under the burden of hope coupled with failure.

That Rodin should have been impelled to give so much of his time and energy to so dark a vision is all the more remarkable because the decade of the 1880s was one of the sunniest in French life and art. In art, the dead hand of the Academy was being lifted; the Impressionists flourished. Monet, Auguste Renoir, Camille Pissarro and others were lightening their palettes and luminously painting the happier sides of France—the graceful streams, the haze of meadows, pleasant holidays, sociable Sundays in blossoming gardens. In this atmosphere of sensory delight, of relaxed pleasures that reflected the bonhomie of the prospering Third Republic, a dour concern with the predicaments of mankind seemed out of place. With a few exceptions the Impressionists were not interested in such topics as they pursued the play of light. The grim mid-century social commentaries of Daumier were out of fashion; the strident spirit of Vincent van Gogh, shaped by poverty and by his ex-

Besides Ghiberti, the poet Charles Baudelaire also influenced Rodin's *Gates of Hell*—both spiritually and philosophically. An admirer of Baudelaire's verses, Rodin sometimes expressed his response to them in the form of quick sketches. In 1888 a Paris publisher who knew of Rodin's interest asked him to illustrate a new edition of Baudelaire's *Les Fleurs du Mal*. The page above is from that edition, and shows a pensive devil poised on one leg next to the poem "All of her" —Baudelaire's passionate reply to the devil's query as to which quality of the poet's beloved he considered the sweetest.

perience in the coal mines of Belgium, had not yet made itself apparent.

The Rodin of *The Gates*, though, was by no means a voice alone in his time. Romanticism was still a force in art and literature, and Rodin by his very temperament was drawn to its pervading melancholy, its concern with the fugitive quality of life and passion, its sense of endless unrest and unresolved search. He found this dark mood expressed, in vivid and evocative language, by several extraordinary poets of 19th Century France. Baudelaire and several who came after him—Paul Verlaine, Jules Laforgue and Arthur Rimbaud—were all poets of disenchantment, disillusioned with the materialistic world around them, troubled by the prevalence of evil in an outwardly contented and comfortable society. In their personal lives they rejected the norms of this society, some resorting to drugs, preferring to exist in twilight states. Today we would call these poets "alienated." In their own era they were lumped together, pejoratively, as "decadents." Baudelaire, the first and greatest of them, was particularly obsessed by the thought of the imminence of decay, of passion spent:

> *O sorrow, sorrow! Time eats life away,*
> *and the obscure Enemy that gnaws at our hearts*
> *fortifies itself on the blood we lose.*

To Rodin, Baudelaire seemed a compelling witness to the uncertainties and hollowness of his times, and the poet exerted an influence upon *The Gates* second only to Dante's. Rodin never met Baudelaire, who died in 1867, when Rodin was still an obscure young decorator's apprentice, but he had come to know his writings well; Baudelaire was the author of a number of scathing reviews of the insipidities in the annual Salons. Rodin closely and repeatedly read Baudelaire's confessional *Flowers of Evil*; in the late 1880s he illustrated a private edition of the poems, with graphic drawings of violence, torture and degradation. He was familiar with Baudelaire's lines:

> *Descend, descend, pitiable victims,*
> *descend the path to eternal hell.*
> *Plunge to the very depths of the gulf where all crimes,*
> *Lashed by a wind not from heaven,*
> *Boil in disorder with a sound of storm.*

In Rodin's eyes, Baudelaire, like Dante, was a prophet of the disintegration of an age, and a judge as well. Therein, perhaps, lies the real key to Rodin's *Gates*. To sit in judgment—wasn't this the highest function of the poet or the artist?

Atop *The Gates* sits and broods Rodin's most celebrated—and most debated—figure, *The Thinker*. He placed it there sometime in the early 1880s. In design it owes a debt to Michelangelo's superhuman forms, especially that of Jeremiah on the ceiling of the Sistine Chapel, and to Carpeaux's version of Ugolino *(page 59)*, of which Rodin owned a cast. But while the paternity of *The Thinker* is not difficult to trace, what is he thinking of? Long afterward Rodin explained that he first conceived of his subject as "Dante, thinking of the plan of his poem." When that idea did not materialize, "I conceived of another thinker, a naked man seated upon a rock, his feet drawn under him, his fist against his teeth, he dreams. The fertile thought slowly elaborates itself within his brain. He is no longer dreamer, he is creator." But again, dreaming what, creating what? When *The Thinker* was first put on public exhibition in 1889, in a cast much enlarged from the figure on the *Gates*, it was entitled *The Poet*. What poet—Dante, Baudelaire? Or, since he had also spoken of *The Thinker* as a "creator," was it possibly Rodin himself?

The more one studies *The Gates*, the more one is drawn to the idea that here is a microcosm made by a dramatist for himself, according to his own rules: he sits above it, pondering his creation. The very structure of the work, with figures moving at various levels of distance within a bold proscenium, suggests a theater, an effect emphasized by the striking play of light on the deeply cut surfaces. Upon this stage Rodin presides, bringing forth, combining and destroying whole casts of characters at will. He is the master, like the Balzac whom he also much admired, of his own *Comédie Humaine*. His work is both a morality play and a repertory theater whose figures changed from year to year, as he replaced one by another.

Among the sculptures Rodin eventually removed from *The Gates* is *The Kiss*. What would such an image of youthful enchantment be doing on so grim a portal in any case? It appears that Rodin initially wanted to present the story of Paolo and Francesca in the happier days of their love as a counterpoint to the later tragedy that beset them. Later he realized that such an idea was unsuitable for *The Gates*, and banished *The Kiss*. After it had embarked on a life of fame of its own, Rodin remarked that while it was "pretty," it was trite: "It is a theme treated according to the tradition of the School: a subject complete in itself and artificially isolated from the world."

So much for the famed *Kiss*, in its maker's estimation. But the very fact that he contemplated a place for it on *The Gates* suggests the presence of an irrepressible streak in Rodin's make-up. Though he had set himself a tragic theme, his robustness kept breaking through. A man of unpredictable impulse, he alternated between grim observation and ebullience. For all his felt kinship with Baudelaire and with the succeeding poets of "decadence" he could not sustain a mood of gloom for long. At times *The Gates* became for him something almost like a pleasure dome through which he roamed happily in pursuit of his changing fantasies. Or, as he himself once expressed it, *The Gates* were a "Noah's Ark" of his inventions.

A typical scene in his studio, when he labored at his masterpiece, bore out this description. The place was alive with pacing models of every age and appearance. He worked from all of them, sometimes from several at a time; but he also worked impulsively, from memory, improvising some gnarled little form while standing on a ladder or perched on a scaffold, marking a position for it on *The Gates*, then descending, squinting up, ordering an assistant to take the figure away for a better try the next day. Sometimes he changed and recombined heads, legs, arms, even whole torsos, male or female. He was much taken with a sturdy Italian girl who posed for his *Eve*—a "panther," he described her. (While working from her figure day by day, Rodin noticed changes in it, and, without realizing that she was pregnant, brought into his statue the suggestion of dawning motherhood.) He hired a weight lifter named Cailloux, who was skilled at lifting bar bells of more than 200 pounds above his head, to pose for his *Adam*. But Rodin also went far beyond his models. The *Crouching Woman* is in a position of torsion that no living person could possibly sustain; in this work Rodin sculpted pathos itself, at its outermost limits.

An aged and haggard woman, her breasts fallen and her flesh decayed, was engaged to pose nude for a work Rodin called *The Old Courtesan*. Reportedly his inspiration for the figure was a ballad by the medieval poet François Villon, in which a wreck of a once-handsome female exclaims, "When I think, alas, of the good days—what I was, what I have become; when I look at my naked body and see myself so changed, dried-out, skinny and shriveled, I almost go out of my mind." The model, far from being an old courtesan herself, was an Italian peasant who had come to visit an artist son in Paris before she died, and was advised to try for a job in Rodin's studio. The sculptor was ever-receptive. "If there is anything more beautiful than a beautiful thing," he said, "it is its ruin."

Rodin's contract called for his portal to be delivered by 1885. It was not, of course, and the irked officials at the Ministry of Fine Arts dispatched more inspectors to the Dépôt des Marbres, then relented to the extent of providing Rodin with more grants. But by the late 1880s it began to dawn on them that Rodin might never complete his commission. The realization may also have struck Rodin himself about then; his inspiration, at first so intense, began to flag. His interests became dispersed. He was especially absorbed with a commission he had received from the mayor and town councilors of Calais, on the Channel coast, to create a civic memorial for the city, a new challenge to his powers of invention. He also found himself involved in projects for monuments to Balzac and to Victor Hugo.

He never finished *The Gates*. It is possible that he never could have. He had set himself a task that was perhaps self-defeating from the start: an exercise in chaos. And Rodin, a man of intuitive pursuits and ever-changing vistas, was hardly one to impose order on chaos. Although drawn like Michelangelo to the grand design, he was temperamentally unfitted for carrying it through to completion. Sometimes, in justification, his defenders would observe that Michelangelo himself had spent 40 years, on and off, sculpting the tomb of Pope Julius II without completing it.

Behind this defensiveness lay his basic feeling that a fragment could be a work of art in itself—perhaps equal to the whole. *The Gates* are one vast fragment, yet more than that. They are a unique storehouse of forms and ideas on which Rodin drew for the rest of his life. They remained in his studio until his death, when, at his wish, they were presented to the French Republic.

A GUIDE TO *THE GATES OF HELL*

The letters superimposed on the photograph at left identify basic architectural features of Rodin's *Gates* mentioned in this chapter and in the following picture essay. The work's main themes and figures are outlined in white, numbered and keyed to the list below. The right-hand numbers below refer to pages on which the reader may see illustrations of Rodin's figures as they appear on *The Gates*, and of separate sculptures in which he treated similar forms or themes.

A: Cornice

B: Tympanum 98-99

C: Left pilaster

D: Right pilaster

E: Left door panel

F: Right door panel

"The Gates of Hell"

Rodin's private vision of the trials and torments of human existence leaps to life in his *Gates of Hell.* Initially inspired by Dante's *Inferno, The Gates* evolved into a panoramic statement of Rodin's own belief that hell is suffered not only by the dead, but by the living; that it is a bleak realm of false goals, lost dreams and unrealized passions. Man, with his pride and hopes, strives for fulfillment only to meet his certain fate—disillusionment and ultimate destruction. Dark as this view is, Rodin invested his creation with an artistic brilliance that both enlightens and enthralls.

The portal, cast in bronze after his death, bears the stamp of almost four decades of effort. Commissioned in 1880 as an entrance to a proposed museum of decorative arts, *The Gates* occupied much of the latter half of Rodin's life. He worked in clay, modeling scores of figures that he cast in plaster and then restlessly rearranged or changed. A number of them also served as the basis for some of his most celebrated separate sculptures.

Rodin never considered *The Gates* completed, but the chaotic look of the work was not altogether unplanned. The sculptor deliberately juxtaposed emerging and receding figures in order to intensify the play of light and shadow that would sustain his grim theme. Yet he also made his forms essentially independent of one another—a haunting reminder that man, in his personal agonies, must finally face them alone.

Rodin's gates are topped by *The Three Shades,* who gesture toward the tumult of sufferers. Below the trio is *The Thinker,* in what appears to be a judgment seat. Around and beneath him is the tossing, writhing cast of characters devised by Rodin. The figures, ranging in size from six inches to four feet, enact their tragedy on a stage that is 21 feet tall and 13 feet wide and nearly 3 feet deep.

The Gates of Hell
OVERALL AND DETAILS FROM "THE GATES" PHOTOGRAPHED AT RODIN MUSEUM, PA

96

Brooding over the doors is Rodin's famous enigma, *The Thinker*. Who is he? Perhaps Rodin himself, a representation of man's ability to reason and to create. As a rational being, *The Thinker* sits as if in judgment of his fellow men—and himself. The very act of thinking generates a tension that vibrates in his body from his scowling brow to his gripping toes. Rodin exercised some artistic license with the figure's powerful musculature. Seen at eye level *The Thinker's* thick shoulders and huge head are out of proportion. He was, however, designed to be viewed from below. From this vantage point his proportions look right.

Above *The Thinker* a frieze of hollow faces proclaims the ghostly presence of lost souls. Behind him, in the tympanum, a dance of death eerily surges from left to right. The arrival of souls in hell is marked by the curved figure of the woman in the upper left-hand corner. The procession continues toward a seething mass of the doomed, some of whom have already collapsed. At the extreme right, a young girl, off balance, shrinks in horror.

Forming a human bridge between the tympanum and the doors is the figure of a falling man. He symbolizes a recurrent theme of *The Gates*—frustration and unfulfilled ambition. With his eyes burned from their sockets, he is Icarus, the mortal who tried to soar to the sun and fell to earth seared and broken.

99

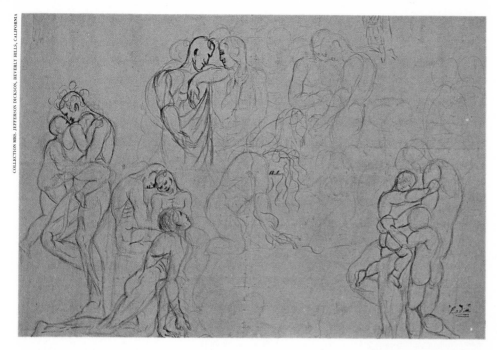

Rodin shared a widespread 19th Century fascination with the tale of Ugolino, a nobleman of medieval Pisa turned traitor, who was imprisoned with his sons, watched them starve, then insanely devoured them. Rodin started sketching Ugolino *(left)* in the 1870s, years before he received his commission for *The Gates.* His study for the Ugolino group *(below)* was cast as a separate bronze in 1882. In *The Gates* it was placed on the left-hand door at eye level *(opposite).* Here the maddened nobleman gropes blindly for his children, a man become beast.

Sketches for Ugolino, 1870s

Ugolino, 1882

Fugit Amor, before 1887

The agony of love unfulfilled is another major theme of *The Gates*. For his inspiration Rodin drew on Dante's tale of Paolo and Francesca, the tragic lovers who were caught and murdered by Francesca's cuckolded husband, and whose souls were consigned to hell. Every pair of lovers on *The Gates* may represent Paolo and Francesca in spirit, but two of the couples are rendered with particularly high drama. In *Fugit Amor*, sometimes called *Fugitive Love* (*left*), the lovers rise from the surface of the portal, their outward thrust a startling enactment of their grief; the sharp angle of the figures allows light and shadow to play

theatrically on their back-to-back bodies. Their hopelessness is emphasized by Paolo's arms, stretching behind him in a desperate attempt to embrace his love. One later version of *Fugit Amor* that was carved in marble (*above*) puts the lovers at a different angle, but their torment remains undiminished.

Placed diagonally to *Fugit Amor* on the left-hand door is yet another representation of Paolo and Francesca (*overleaf*). As in *Fugit Amor*, Paolo, his face a mask of sorrow, reaches vainly for Francesca but she seems to be sliding away, literally slipping from his grasp.

103

Rodin called *The Gates of Hell* his "Noah's Ark," the vessel he populated with the creatures of his imagination. Indeed, the project was the focal point of his art for many years. Its main subjects inspired both smaller works on the portal itself and separate pieces. The male lover in *Fugit Amor (page 102)* was slightly redesigned by Rodin in a smaller, less dominant version for the lower part of the right-hand door *(above, left)*. His outstretched body conceals his beloved. This same figure was also made into an individual study, a kneeling supplicant titled *The Prodigal (page 84)*. On the left pilaster of *The Gates* an old courtesan *(above, right)*,

partially covered by a grieving younger woman, is shown as the pathetic victim of a life devoted to carnal pleasures. She raises her cadaverous face plaintively upward, her body sagging and flaccid. In a separate bronze made of her *(page 108)* Rodin lowered her head, depicting her as if her eyes were unable to stray from the gruesome sight of her own spent body. Her flesh, marked with hollows and highlights, reveals the ravages of her wanton existence. Yet the work radiates Rodin's romantic admiration for the magnificent ruin of a once-beautiful figure.

The man shown falling from the tympanum *(pages 98-*

99) is repeated at the top of the right pilaster, but now he clutches at a crouching woman perched over him *(above, left)*. Rodin combined the two figures in a freestanding bronze to produce the dynamic *"I am beautiful" (page 109)*. The title comes from a line in a poem by Baudelaire: "I am as beautiful, oh mortals, as a dream in stone." The words are the cry of an artist who has spent his days seeking beauty: he holds it for a tantalizing moment but is denied the ultimate joy of physical union. Rodin, as he often did, portrayed beauty in the form of a voluptuous woman, the object of man's desire and the ultimate cause of his fall.

The admiration Rodin felt for the female figure finds no better manifestation than in the sensuous arch of the back of the girl who appears to fling herself into the mass of bodies in the tympanum *(above, right)*. Rodin reproduced this abandoned female attitude in the tender *Eternal Springtime (page 110)*. And in 1909, when he was 69, Rodin returned to a similar study of the torso of his original model and had an abstracted, enlarged version of it cast in bronze *(page 111)*. The head, arms and legs were removed; Rodin deemed them needless distractions from the graceful curve of the back and felt that the fragment should be considered complete.

The Old Courtesan, 1885

"I am beautiful" 1882

Eternal Springtime, 188

Torso of a Young Woman, 190

RODIN MUSEUM, PARIS

V

A Trio
of Humiliations

Beginning in the mid-1880s Rodin found himself not only a sculptor of some repute but the center of raging controversy over three major projects he was asked to undertake. The commissions were as varied as their sponsors. The first came from the Channel port of Calais, which invited Rodin to memorialize an act of civic heroism in the Middle Ages; the next was from the French government itself, for a statue of Victor Hugo, who had recently died; the third was from the Société des Gens de Lettres, a large Paris organization of writers, for a statue of Hugo's great literary contemporary Honoré de Balzac. All three commissions honored but also challenged Rodin, and all led to protracted embroilments between sponsors and sculptor. There were fracases over money, demands for changes in the figures, objections, recriminations and threats. The culminating furor—over the *Balzac*—at times seemed to involve the entire French public.

The Burghers of Calais (pages 126-133), begun in 1884 and finished by 1889, was so bedeviled by local dissension, as well as by the city's laggard fund raising for its installation, that the work was not put in place until 1895. The *Hugo (page 134)* was rejected out of hand as unfit for the Panthéon, the mausoleum of France's great men that it was supposed to have graced. The *Balzac*—the work that Rodin considered "the sum of my whole life . . . my great discovery" *(page 139)*—was also turned down by its infuriated sponsors, and did not find a public site in Paris until 1939.

Although ever ready for controversy, Rodin was not one to seek it. While he wanted to break away from conventional standards, he never felt the urge to deliberately shock. For all his brusque and headstrong air, he was so thin-skinned that he suffered torments when a confrontation came and harsh words flew: the wounds from *The Age of Bronze* took years to heal. Still, with the gathering momentum of his powers of invention and his rising pride of self-assertion, such encounters were bound to occur. In retrospect it is possible to find comedy in some of these clashes: men of solid demeanor engaged him and then, as the extraordinary imagination they had hired came into play, charged him

EARLY STUDIES FOR *THE BURGHERS*

For *The Burghers of Calais* Rodin made dozens of studies, fashioning nude figures first, then sculpting them draped. The early plaster figures below and on the opposite page range in size from just over a foot to 28 inches in height. Even in small studies like these, Rodin was able to incorporate an astonishing number of individual details, but he was never satisfied. He continued to make changes as he enlarged the models, first to half life size and ultimately to figures more than six feet tall.

with betrayal. They might have realized from the outset that Rodin, once given rein, was a man full of surprises, and that an artist capable of an *Ugolino* or an *Old Courtesan* as well as *The Kiss* might be capable of anything.

The Calais affair started peaceably enough. When Rodin, always alert to the possibilities of a large project, learned from a friend in Calais that its officials were considering a memorial to the finest hour of their city's past, he leaped at the chance; here was something not only with a patriotic theme but with the medieval motif he especially loved. He invited the city's mayor, Omer Dewavrin, to his studio to see his work. The mayor was so enthralled that he was of a mind to give Rodin the commission on the spot. But first he had to clear matters with the Calais monument committee.

The project had been contemplated for decades but held up because of local indecision and lack of funds. Every Calais school child knew the story it was intended to celebrate, as told by the 14th Century chronicler Froissart. In 1347, after the disastrous French defeat at Crécy at the hands of Edward III of England in the Hundred Years' War, the city of Calais had defiantly withstood almost a year's siege, only to succumb at last. Edward then demanded his price for the cessation of hostilities: the execution of any six prominent citizens of Calais. At that point six leading burghers volunteered to give up their lives. Headed by the city's most revered elder, Eustache de Saint-Pierre, and by Mayor Jean d'Aire, they presented themselves to the King and offered themselves to his executioners. Edward wanted to kill them, but so noble was their bearing—and so did their brave gesture of sacrifice move his queen—that he spared them and the city as well.

The monument that Rodin executed—some observers deem it his best work—reflects the proud legend, but with certain significant alterations. Sculpted in the vivid, rough-surfaced style that was Rodin's hallmark, the six burghers advance toward their fateful meeting with Edward—a monarch not noted for compassion—in a complex agony of attitudes. They are heroic, but they are also frightened. One burgher looks back despairingly toward his mourning townsmen, another clutches at his head in despair, still another expresses anguish by the flexed tension of his body and hands. All are nonetheless doing what nobility of soul compels them to do, moving toward their dread destination—moved by courage (and by the sculptor's skill in conveying motion). The effect Rodin produced is not one of "grace under pressure," as Ernest Hemingway defined courage; it is of sheer heroism.

Rodin's work, however, did not express heroism as the 19th Century burghers of Calais expected it to be expressed. What the mayor and his committeemen had had in mind was one symbolic figure to represent the event: that of the eldest of the heroes, Eustache de Saint-Pierre, possibly surrounded by allegorical shapes denoting Civic Ardor and so forth. But Rodin had read Froissart carefully—especially the passage which describes the six men, trailed by the weeping populace, setting off to the English camp in the manner stipulated by the King: "bareheaded, barefooted, with halters around their necks, and the keys to the city and castle in their hands." Here was a drama, Rodin thought, that should not be reduced to a single, formal figure, but that should be presented on a sculptural stage with the six burghers playing their separate parts, each conveying the individuality of his suffering, while all moved together to meet their fate.

Rodin's decision to make the six men equals in his composition marked the beginning of his boldest sculptural conception after *The Gates of Hell*, and the beginning also of his difficulties with the committeemen of Calais. Shortly after his meeting with Mayor Dewavrin he dashed off a letter indicating that something unusual might be in the making: "Ever since I had the honor of your visit I have been taken up with the monument and have hit upon an idea that appeals to me. . . . I have never seen a scheme better suited to its subject or more completely original. . . . I have just made a model in clay and had it cast [in plaster]. . . . The subject is heroic and calls for heroic treatment and the group of six figures sacrificing themselves is imbued with communicative emotion." Perhaps to offset the somewhat casual mention of six figures, Rodin added reassuringly that "the figure of Eustache de Saint-Pierre, by his dignity of gesture, leads and unites his companions."

Calais was not reassured. Six diverse figures on one pedestal? A proper monument, by 19th Century convention, was supposed to consist of just one figure or at least one dominating figure. The committeemen were perturbed, although perhaps attracted by the thought of getting six figures for the price of one. The first small sketches they saw, showing a huddle of forms, also puzzled them. But Mayor Dewavrin appears to have argued persuasively that when his new friend Rodin completed his figures they would be statuesque and dignified, in keeping with a civic memorial. So Rodin was commissioned to proceed—with the proviso that his advanced models must be approved by the committee before he received a final go-ahead, and that they should eventually be "finished and perfected with the same care as that given to works accepted by the annual Salon." Rodin was given 15,000 francs; for the cost of the bronze cast and of the pedestal, the added sum of 20,000 francs was to come later.

This was surely insurance. But when the Calais committeemen saw one of Rodin's advanced models in 1885, they were outraged. "This is not the way in which we had visualized our glorious forbears as they made their way to the English camp," a spokesman wrote Rodin. "Their dejected attitude offends our religion. The group leaves much to be desired in respect to elegance." Even the details were wrong: "The monotony and stiffness of the outlines should be broken by varying the sizes of the six figures. . . . We note that Eustache de Saint-Pierre is dressed in a thickly folded material rather than in the thin garments recorded in the history of the event." The committee demanded that Rodin remake the group.

Rodin exploded. Elegance indeed! That was the last thing he was out to attain. And alter the attitudes, change the sizes, perhaps make a pretty little pyramid of figures? Who were these petty people to presume to dictate to him? Back to Calais went a letter denouncing the demands as

threatening to "emasculate my work." He would not hear of adapting his figures to meet convention—one which "since the beginning of our century has been directly opposed to those of preceding ones, and which has imposed coldness and lack of movement upon works conceived under it." Rodin indicated, in short, that he was ready to drop the project. But his hauteur, coupled with the support of Mayor Dewavrin (of whom Rodin soon made one of his grateful busts), saved the day. The committeemen let him go ahead for the time being, although, as Rodin observed, "They would have preferred gestures *à la Marseillaise!*"—a reference to Rude's panoply of theatrically heroic figures adorning the Arc de Triomphe in Paris.

As he went ahead, Rodin's own concept grew and changed, just as it did with *The Gates.* The idea he developed, however, was more coherent than that of *The Gates.* In *The Burghers,* he finally decided, he would emphasize the theme of individual suffering for a collective noble aim. Gradually, he worked at differentiating the six figures and giving each its own characteristics. Over the next four years *The Burghers* evolved into something far more dramatic than Rodin himself at first had imagined. Part of the succession of his gnarled, often fragmentary working models can be seen today in the Rodin Museum in Meudon outside Paris. Visitors who make their way there confront a chronicle of the evolution of a concept. To see it is as absorbing in its way as it would be to see Proust's innumerable changes on the page proofs of a novel or Beethoven's sketchbooks for an emerging symphony.

At the outset—as the committeemen of Calais first encountered them —the burghers are a rudimentary cluster. Next come little clay studies of individuals: first in the nude, to define their basic posture, then with shreds of garments on them—shadowy draperies, recalling the medieval sculptural tradition of the robe as virtually a skin encasing the spiritual body. Next the figures are shown linked by ropes. Within this unity, however, they reflect an increasing contrast of bearing. Each has his personal response—an attitude of resignation here, a sad farewell there. Each man moves at a pace of his own, alone with his thoughts, yet all are in a rhythmic circular movement that suggests nothing so much as a dance of death. Through their various stages of creation the burghers become a scenic unfolding, a narrative, Rodin's greatest exercise with movement and time. As you walk around them you find yourself momentarily seeing them as one figure in a sequence of motion; but when you look again you know better. Each figure is both kin to the next and isolated, an island unto himself with his conscience: the feet drag, the hands are tortured, each body struggles for life—and with its soul as well.

Froissart's chronicle had not described the looks or demeanor of the six burghers. But Rodin sensed that he needed models quite different from the usual athletic studio types. His concept called for male models who bore marks and scars of suffering—such as he had portrayed in *The Man with the Broken Nose*—but whose faces and bodies also suggested spirituality, character, pride. Rodin's friend the painter Alphonse Legros, a bearded man of Gothic appearance, is thought to have posed for Eustache de Saint-Pierre, and another painter friend, Jean-Charles Cazin, for one of the other burghers. Ironically, Rodin also used his own son as a model. By now Auguste was almost a derelict, unable to hold a job, given to wandering around; he would appear at his father's door whenever he needed a free meal or a handout. Rodin sometimes called him in, for a pittance, to serve as man of all work about the studio. Auguste posed for the figure of the burgher standing next to Eustache de Saint-Pierre, holding the key to Calais.

By 1889 Rodin felt that *The Burghers* merited public display. He included the work in the two-man show with Monet put on at the Georges Petit Gallery, and a few months later he exhibited a cast of one of the figures at the Universal Exposition. The acclaim he won impressed the committeemen of Calais at least temporarily; they put on a lottery to raise the funds needed to complete the project. But collections were meager, and meanwhile Rodin came up with a culminating idea for *The Burghers* that enraged its sponsors anew. He decided to eliminate the high pedestal on which sculptural groupings were traditionally placed, and to substitute what amounted to no more than a thick slab. In thus bringing *The Burghers* almost down to ground level Rodin had a purpose; it was, as he later explained, to "allow the public to penetrate to the heart of the subject." He wanted viewers to rub shoulders with the figures, even to have children clamber over them.

The very notion shocked Calais. A monument without a stand on which to place it, and without a railing around it? Rodin had obviously gone mad. He would have to yield on these points if he hoped to have the work accepted. A protracted battle of wills ensued, and the committeemen finally won out. In 1895 *The Burghers*—incongruously placed on a high platform resembling an immense sarcophagus, and surrounded by an equally incongruous cast-iron railing—was duly unveiled at Calais before a concourse of officials and citizens. Rodin did not prevail even in his choice of a site for his work. He had wanted it installed in the heart of Calais, in the square before the Town Hall, where people would pass it every day. Instead, it was erected in front of a public garden, amid the distractions of tall trees. Almost three decades passed before it was brought down to earth and removed to the site Rodin had envisioned for it.

Rodin was bruised by his experiences with *The Burghers*. He lacked the urbanity that might have enabled him to shrug off what he considered to be abuse. Dour and stubborn by nature, he was not disposed to yield once set on a chosen path; he tended to fight back grimly, to try to dislodge his patrons and critics from their prejudices. This always exhausted him emotionally, and in the case of the lengthy squabbling over *The Burghers* his frame of mind was not improved by a growing disorder in his personal affairs.

He was, to be sure, buoyed by the recognition that came his way as a result of the exhibit of his work at the Petit Gallery and at the Universal Exposition in 1889. He could not help but be pleased by a further mark of recognition that year: his invitation to join the jury that judged entries for the Salon. But professional triumph was tempered by private trou-

At top is a postcard view of *The Burghers of Calais* as the monument was unveiled outside a Calais park in 1895—mounted on a formidable stone pedestal and surrounded by an ornate iron railing. Slightly damaged by a shell fragment during World War I, the two-ton sculpture was removed to a cellar for safekeeping. With the peace, it was replaced in its original setting, but after five years was installed as Rodin had wished it to be—minus a railing and on its own low pedestal in front of the medieval Town Hall of Calais.

CABINET DES ESTAMPES, BIBLIOTHÈQUE NATIONALE, PARIS

Rodin became interested in engraving on a visit to London, where his painter-friend Alphonse Legros was teaching graphic techniques. Back in Paris he executed a number of dry points, including the portraits of Victor Hugo above. As may be seen by comparing them with the photograph below, they are excellent likenesses. Rodin based these engravings on preparatory sketches for a bust he sculpted during Hugo's last years of life. Hugo's impatience as a sitter caused Rodin to work at a pace unusual even for him. He turned out hundreds of quick studies, sketching so rapidly that he sometimes went through his drawing pad and had to resort to using cigarette papers.

ble. As he entered his fifties—an age when most men are content to settle back into the safety of domestic routine—Rodin was distractedly juggling a double life.

He decided to move Rose out of Paris to a house at Bellevue, in the Seine valley. There were moments when Rodin enjoyed staying there, sketching in his seven-windowed attic retreat or bargaining for tomatoes with a neighbor. But there were less pleasant moments as well, involving his frequent absences in the city. Rose was well aware of the reason for them. Lonely and bitter—she called herself "a sailor's wife" —she would pace the garden night after night, waiting for Rodin to arrive on the late riverboat from Paris. Understandably, she was outspoken in her outrage over his infidelity; she may have been illiterate but she was by no means inarticulate. Arriving at Bellevue was more often than not a trial for Rodin.

Camille, too, was becoming increasingly annoyed about his divided attentions. She and Rodin shared a place in Paris—an old villa he had leased behind a garden off the Boulevard d'Italie, where George Sand and Alfred de Musset had also once lived as lovers. Rodin thought he was sure of Camille, but other, younger men—the composer Claude Debussy among them—were being drawn to her. Her manner was vivacious, her looks so radiant that the critic Edmond de Goncourt recorded them in his journal; at one party, he took pains to write, she shone in a "bodice embroidered with large Japanese flowers."

Troubled, torn, yet filled with unquenchable vitality, Rodin restlessly moved from project to project in one or another of his studios. In 1890 he put the final touches on a work he had had under way simultaneously with *The Burghers*, and one that proved just as thankless. This work was a monument to Victor Hugo, commissioned by the French government in 1886, the year after Hugo died, and it was intended to stand outside the entrance to the Panthéon. Not long before his death the grand old man of French letters had reluctantly consented to let Rodin make a bust of him. He was impatient at the whole idea, and Rodin had had to hover about while he worked, talked or ate, then dash off to sketch what he had seen on paper or in clay, then pop back in to refresh his observations. For all these obstacles Rodin thought Hugo a magnificent person, "a French Jupiter," and when he received the commission for the Panthéon he rose eagerly to the challenge.

This time, however, his far-reaching imagination betrayed him. As if to enliven the somber aura of the Panthéon, with its august memorials, Rodin decided to depict Hugo not as a heroic figure standing alone, but as the Poet reclining nude amid a bevy of female nudes. Supposedly they were muses from whom Hugo was receiving inspiration, but in their appearance they were more like nymphs or sea sirens. The fact that Hugo kept a mistress, and that he was at least Rodin's match in his weakness for women, added pungence to the notion. In the model Rodin submitted for approval in 1890, three muses hover over Hugo while he has a finger at his lips as if saying "Tut-tut." The governmental jury appointed to pass on this work promptly found Rodin's lush design unsuitable for the nation's most venerated shrine; as one juror dryly observed, it was architecturally at odds with the setting. Perhaps he would try again? Rodin went on designing further versions of his *Hugo*, "naked like a god . . . seated among the rocks, beaten by the waves." Not one of them, with or without attending muses, was deemed worthy of the site. The satisfaction Rodin was to derive from this project was scant indeed; two decades after he received the commission a marble version of a solitary *Hugo* was erected at a safe distance from the Panthéon —in the gardens of the Palais Royal.

The unfortunate *Hugo* was not so much a case of Rodin's conflict with official taste as of a lapse of his own. His self-discipline still had a way of suddenly deserting him, just as it had in his younger days. The *Hugo* was not the only example of Rodin's failure of judgment in these years of artistic maturity. Another was a monument he concocted to the 17th Century landscape painter Claude Lorrain at the behest of a committee formed to commemorate the great native artist of Lorraine in the provincial capital of Nancy. Rodin's design was an improbable one of a wispy man atop a huge pedestal from which mythological steeds burst forth. Had he forgotten his opposition to pedestals? And what were prancing horses doing in a memorial to a placid, pastoral painter? When the work was at last unveiled in the presence of the President of the Republic, the good people of Nancy were so offended and incensed —especially by the horses, which they thought misshapen—that they surged toward the monument spewing invective, and a large-scale riot was barely averted.

Rodin had had his fill of controversy when, in 1891, he received the commission to make the memorial to Balzac. In this instance, he assumed, he would be free of quibbles and quarrels about his work; his hope was based in part on the fact that he had been chosen for the task at the instigation of the president of the sponsoring group—France's most famous living writer, Émile Zola. Zola was not only the author of *Nana* and many other novels of uncompromising realism, but a supporter of all that was liberal and new in the arts in general. Surely there would be no trouble here with nonconformist sculpture. Rodin's letter of acceptance to his benefactor showed his excitement and his conviction that he was in good hands: "Mon cher Maître: Thanks to you, I find myself the sculptor of Balzac and the protégé of Émile Zola. I am placed in a redoubtable position." Soon he also found himself in a most disagreeable one.

The sponsor of the memorial was the Société des Gens de Lettres —the Society of Men of Letters. Its founding had been Balzac's idea, but despite that fact and Zola's prestigious leadership it was less an honorific group than a kind of trade association—an authors' league primarily concerned with practical matters like copyrights and contracts. It embraced men of many degrees of talent and shades of opinion. It was not, except in name, a union of knowledgeable intellectuals predisposed to look with favor on artistic innovations.

The Society's first choice for a sculptor for the Balzac memorial was not Rodin but Henri Chapu, an older and more conventional artist. Chapu died in 1891 without having gotten very far on the project, and a successor was needed. A number of Rodin's friends (perhaps spurred by Rodin himself) approached Zola and the Society, proposing him as the logical choice. Zola liked the idea and suggested that Rodin personally express his interest; Rodin promptly did so. There was, of course, one of those infernal judging committees to be consulted. Zola assured its members that Rodin was "one of the best sculptors of the time." A conservative faction preferred one Marquet de Vasselot, but Rodin won by a committee vote of 12 to 8. In his eagerness, when the contract awarding him an advance of 10,000 francs was signed, he promised to finish the statue in 18 months—a rash act, as he soon realized.

How to represent Balzac, titan of the French novel? No more allegories, no more tricked-out accouterments: Rodin had perhaps learned a lesson from his *Claude Lorrain*. Nor would any idealized, reverential portrait serve. Although Balzac had died in 1850, when Rodin was only 10, Rodin did not view him as from a long distance, with awe. On the contrary, he felt a kinship with Balzac, the creator of immense projects, the herculean artist concerned with the entire range of human passions, the searching commentator on the mores and destinies of men. (Also like Rodin, Balzac had been a maker of occasional potboilers and a heroic womanizer.) But there was a problem in memorializing Balzac realistically. Unlike the majestic Hugo, he had been a tub of a man—squat, with an enormous paunch and short legs, his features gross and swollen. So, at least, the few surviving daguerreotypes and caricatures represented him. There was a danger that too much realism might do little service to Balzac's memory.

Casting about for accounts by contemporaries, Rodin came across the poet Alphonse Lamartine's description of Balzac's face as "an element"—a force of nature—and of a bearing so grand that it overcame obesity: "There was so much soul that it carried him lightly; the weight seemed to give him force, not take it away from him." Here Rodin found the genesis for a scheme. He decided that he must, without belying appearances, extract the elemental man within, and even make a virtue of Balzac's deformities.

Rodin went to other sources as well. He traveled to Touraine, Balzac's home province, seeking similar facial and bodily types. He even found a tailor who had once cut clothes for Balzac and got his exact measurements. This in turn raised another problem: how should Balzac be presented? Nude—which might emphasize his bulbousness—or clothed, and if clothed, how? Not in anything like a toga surely: but would a frock coat not seem just as much of an artifice? Rodin experimented with both approaches, making more than 40 preliminary studies, many of which are also preserved in the cabinets of the museums at Paris and Meudon. In one series Balzac is seen proudly naked, athletic, sometimes flexed with mighty muscles, sometimes with huge arms folded on his chest and legs spread apart challengingly, as if awaiting combat. In another series the figure is molded as a massive shape with a rough cloak thrown over it; Rodin had learned that Balzac was accustomed to working in a loose dressing gown.

All these preparatory studies took time. When Rodin's deadline for delivery of the statue came and passed, he had nothing ready to show the Society. A clamor arose to see just what he was doing or not doing. When the Society's annoyed envoys were finally admitted to his studio in the summer of 1893 they were taken aback. They saw a raw clay model of what seemed an obscenely naked, gross, potbellied wrestler. Word spread fast through the Society of the freakish absurdity, and the newspaper *Le Figaro* carried an item about Rodin's "strange" creation. Rodin pleaded for more time, while Zola urged forbearance on his colleagues.

By the spring of 1894 there was still no *Balzac*. Zola had been succeeded in the Society by another president who was inclined to sympathize with Rodin, but the conservative faction was nearing the end of its patience. Again a delegation called on Rodin, and came away even more affronted. What its members had been shown was a *Balzac* clothed, or at least draped, but so crudely and limply that the entire work seemed to them, as they reported to their colleagues, "an unformed mass . . . a colossal fetus." A move began in the Society to sue Rodin for default and to recover the advance he had been paid; at one point he received a rude summons to deliver a completed statue within 24 hours—an order that was rescinded through the intervention of the Society's more liberal members. Rodin was exhausted and depressed. Edmond de Goncourt, who met him on a train going from Paris to the country, found him "really changed and very melancholy on account of his low state and the fatigue he felt from his work. . . . He complained almost distressingly of the vexations which . . . are inflicted on artists by art committees."

The chief source for the likeness of Balzac that Rodin needed for his monument to the great novelist was this photograph made in 1842, when Balzac was in his forties. Below is a dressing gown made posthumously to Balzac's measurements by his old tailor at Rodin's behest. Stiffened with plaster, it was kept in Rodin's studio for reference use in the final version of the Balzac memorial.

Nevertheless, Rodin pressed on. To stave off those in the Society who wanted to foreclose on him he surrendered his 10,000-franc advance as a bond, and again pleaded for time: "I ask that you allow me the means of honoring, to the limits of my powers and my will, the great man whose example must inspire you all." He was granted another postponement while he labored on, trying innumerable variants of the *Balzac*. The talk in Paris was malicious; people scoffed that Rodin, who had not completed *The Gates of Hell*, was incapable of finishing anything. In 1896 his foes in the Society launched a scheme to get rid of him once and for all and replace him with Vasselot, the polished Academician who had lost out to him in the original competition by only four votes. Yet Rodin managed to win still another two years of grace. A final figure, at long last, was about to emerge from the enclosure of the Dépôt des Marbres. This version, although still strange and repulsive to some who saw it, was more complete. With misgivings, the Society agreed to let Rodin exhibit it in public for the first time at the approaching Salon of 1898.

For a while it seemed that Rodin would not meet even this commitment. Suddenly friends heard that he was on the verge of collapse, utterly desolated—and for a reason wholly apart from the *Balzac* imbroglio. One night in 1898 Camille Claudel walked out of his life for good. The reason may be buried in the mountains of papers and letters —Rodin never threw anything away—that are preserved in the Rodin

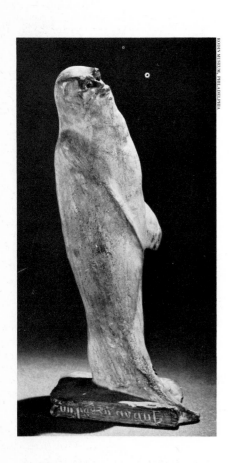

Amid the derisive public laughter over Rodin's *Balzac*, a Parisian souvenir manufacturer produced this nine-inch plaster parody of the statue, presenting the novelist in the guise of a seal. Inscribed on the figurine's base are the words "One Step Forward," a mocking reference both to Balzac's pose and to Rodin's pre-eminence among the sculptors of the day.

Museum in Paris, and that scholars have never been permitted to examine. The most likely theory is that Camille tried and failed to persuade him to leave Rose for her.

Rodin never talked about the rupture. Once, in later years, his biographer Judith Cladel pressed him on the subject, saying: "But it is said that you [and Camille] have four children." Rodin's enigmatic reply was: "If that were so my duty would have been only too clear." A guess as to the real cause of the break is possible. Forced to choose between the two women in his life, Rodin may ultimately have preferred subservience and domesticity to brilliance and tempestuousness; perhaps he wanted to preserve his energies for fighting with art committees. Perhaps also the matter of loyalty counted; Rose had shared those difficult early years when only she and Rodin believed that he was going to do great things. Camille, for her part, is never known to have offered any light on the affair. After she left Rodin she had a nervous breakdown and became a recluse, living in a small, sparsely furnished flat that grew increasingly dirty and littered. Without her knowledge, Rodin arranged several showings of her sculpture and bought some of the exhibited works. He also sent emissaries to see her, but the mere mention of his name threw her into a rage. In 1913 she was removed to an institution and died there 30 years later.

The first shock of her departure from Rodin's life was mere prelude to the trial he had to endure when the *Balzac* appeared at the Salon of 1898. Howls of outrage and hoots of laughter greeted it. The more than 2,000 visitors who swarmed around it in the very first hours of the opening day saw a larger-than-life-sized plaster, beaten and incised by what seemed an unusually violent hand, of a looming, spectral colossus, cloaked, weighty, distended, the masklike head thrown back as if in a moment of defiance touched with revelation. Many viewers felt that Rodin was simply playing a joke on the public. The outcry in the press was furious. What he believed to be his masterpiece was vilified as "a snowman," "an obscenity," "a toad in a sack," "this lump of plaster, kicked together by a lunatic," and proof of the "degree of mental aberration we have reached" at the end of the 19th Century. Caricatures of the *Balzac* were hawked on the boulevards. An art dealer gave a masked ball at which he received his guests garbed in a burlesque of it. The Society of Men of Letters, hurrying for cover, disavowed the sculpture, announcing that it did not recognize it as the statue of Balzac it had commissioned.

Yet Rodin still had friends and partisans—an increasing number, indignant at such treatment of him. Georges Clemenceau, the future Premier of France, excoriated the Society in his newspaper *L'Aurore*. A manifesto in Rodin's defense was drawn up and signed by a wide array of notables—Clemenceau, Zola, Anatole France, Claude Debussy, the painters Monet, Signac and Toulouse-Lautrec, the rising sculptors Aristide Maillol and Antoine Bourdelle, and many others. A public subscription was launched to buy the *Balzac* for the city of Paris for 30,000 francs, the price the Society was to have paid. The *Balzac* became a *cause célèbre* second only to the Dreyfus affair, which was then still raging. This was the year in which the infamous Major Esterhazy was tried for the betrayal of military secrets for which Captain Dreyfus had been unjustly found guilty and sentenced to life imprisonment on Devil's Island. It was also the year in which Zola, who had championed Dreyfus and tried to expose Esterhazy, was himself condemned to jail for his activity. Among intellectuals, the alignments on either side of the *Balzac* affair coincided, in all their harshness and vindictiveness, with those of the Dreyfus affair. The liberal Dreyfusards favored Rodin's work; the conservative anti-Dreyfusards opposed it.

Rodin, who was wholly uninterested in politics, was frightened by the uproar. To Monet, who wrote him an admiring letter about the *Balzac*, he effusively replied that such appreciation gave him "strength," and added: "I've had a mass of letters like the ones you had when it was the fashion to laugh at your invention of putting breezes in landscapes." Hostile mail was only one of his concerns; he was also disturbed by the fact that most of those who had contributed to the subscription for the statue were in the Dreyfus camp, and he made the mistake of saying so to a writer who worked for *L'Aurore*. This provoked a stiff note from the newspaper's editor, Clemenceau, to the fund's chairman: "M. Rodin told a member of the staff of *L'Aurore* that he was afraid of having too many of Zola's friends among the contributors to the *Balzac* fund. Kindly remove my name from the list in your possession."

Despite this barb, Rodin was determined not to prolong the controversy over the *Balzac*. He withdrew it from the Salon and announced that he was going to keep it for himself. Eventually he set it up in the garden of the house he had bought at Meudon, where it remained to the end of his years. Though plaster casts of it were periodically shown elsewhere in Europe, he resisted all offers for its purchase. Finally, only two months before World War II, a bronze cast of *Balzac* was installed, with civic blessings, at the corner of the Boulevards Raspail and Montparnasse, on the Left Bank in Paris.

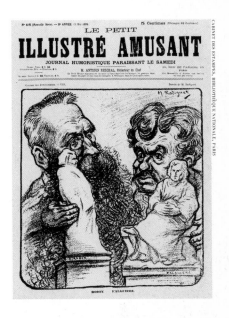

The May 1899 issue of a humor magazine published in Paris carried the cover above, showing a confrontation between Rodin and Alexandre Falguiere, the sculptor who was asked to take on the Balzac project after Rodin's statue was found wanting. To quash rumors of their rivalry, the two friends sculpted portraits of each other, which by mutual agreement they exhibited at the Salon of 1899. The photograph below shows Rodin working on the Falguière bust.

At the time of its rejection by the Society, Rodin had tried to be philosophical. "Esthetic lawmakers are against my *Balzac*, also the majority of the public and the press. What does it matter? The statue will make its own way into people's minds." This, again, took time. It was Rodin's most radical work—the one that showed the least debt or linkage to the past. A few years later, when tempers had cooled, he tried to explain the look of the *Balzac*. "In his opinion," the interviewer reported, "the statue of a man celebrated for his heart and mind should not be a representation of his body, but a sort of construction whose lines should express the soul of the man. . . . The *Balzac* is a kind of dolmen or granite menhir, a stone arched in a movement of disdainful pride, which expresses the whole character of Balzac. . . . It is indeed a monument; it is not a 'monsieur' reproduced in stone."

Still, there is reason to believe that Rodin was not quite satisfied with his *Balzac*, and that he thought of tinkering with it further, as if his seven years of labor on it had not been sufficient time. Had he gone too far, or possibly not far enough? In any event, he never again attempted a work of such scope.

Maker of Monuments

In Rodin's day a sculptor's chief ambition was to win commissions for large public monuments. The competition was often fierce, but the fees were large, fame was almost certain, and above all the opportunity beckoned to create works on a grand scale. These considerations motivated Rodin to seek such commissions even though he was building a reputation as a skilled producer of portraits, Salon pieces and decorative art.

Through his own energetic efforts, and with the help of friends, he succeeded in securing a number of important assignments, including a memorial to the heroes of medieval Calais and monuments to the two literary giants of 19th Century France, Victor Hugo and Honoré de Balzac. But these projects were uniformly destined to end in frustration, and—so far as their sponsors were concerned—in failure. Unable to conform to conventional standards, unwilling to curb his fertile imagination to satisfy the demands of monument committees, Rodin created works that were never fully appreciated in his lifetime. As he once said, "When one is preoccupied with pleasing that million-headed monster called 'the public,' one loses one's personality and independence. . . . I know very well that one must fight, for one is often in contradiction to the spirit of the age." Out of his personal struggle came two of his greatest achievements, perhaps the last truly monumental sculptures of the human figure —*The Burghers of Calais* and *Balzac*.

Among Rodin's early monument designs was one intended to commemorate the Franco-Prussian War of 1870. Although the composition was based on an acceptable theme—the spirit of France rallying her forces—the judging committee rejected Rodin's treatment. Perhaps the frenzied appeal of the winged figure and the jagged contortions of the wounded soldier reminded committee members too painfully of France's humiliating defeat.

Call to Arms, 1879
RODIN MUSEUM, PARIS

Sketch for *The Burghers of Calais*, plaster, 1884

Rodin's first major public monument, begun in 1884, enmeshed him in a decade of bitter controversy with its sponsor, the city of Calais. The theme was the heroism of six citizens who, in 1347, volunteered their lives to England's Edward III in order to save their city from devastation. Both the event and the medieval era in which it took place fascinated Rodin.

The plaster sketch which he first submitted to the Calais monument committee showed his preliminary concept of six men grouped together on a conventional wedding-cake type of pedestal *(above)*. But as he worked, Rodin decided to eliminate the pedestal so that the viewer could respond more directly to each brave martyr's individual reaction to impending death.

127

OVERALL AND DETAILS FROM "THE BURGHERS OF CALAIS" PHOTOGRAPHED AT JOSEPH H. HIRSHHORN COLLECTION

Dressed in loose robes and wearing thick rope halters around their necks as a sign of acceptance of bondage, the six grim burghers of Calais prepare to meet their fate. Two of them carry keys to the town's gates and citadel in final surrender to the English besiegers they had so long resisted. Acting to prevent the certain slaughter of their townsmen, the burghers offer their own lives.

Characteristically, Rodin refused to picture this story in the kind of high-blown allegory of Fortitude and Courage usually expected in such monuments. Rather, he wanted to reveal the true range of emotions he imagined the men had experienced. Rodin knew that no man, however brave or noble, goes to his death easily. Thus, the burghers do not march steadfastly to their doom; there is no comradely linking of arms or head-high stride toward the enemy. Perceptively, Rodin even shows some of the men turning in fear from their awful destination. Here is the heart of the drama: the instant when each man makes the decision to commit himself.

By positioning the figures as he did—the result of months of experiment—and by endowing them with a variety of gestures, Rodin subtly leads the viewer around the group, to experience each figure individually. (On the following pages are faces from the other side of the group.)

Rodin believed that "to model shadows is to create thoughts." A difficult concept to imagine, it comes brilliantly clear when one stands beside *The Burghers.* The deep, vertical shadows of the drapery, for example, seem to weigh down the figures, generating a sense of pathos and doom. The skillful modeling of the flesh is also evocative. The impulse to touch the bronze is great: as Albert Elsen, a leading Rodin scholar, has written, "If one runs a finger along the arm of a burgher and then on his own, the burgher's seems more richly complex." It is this richness of surface, the hollows and ridges that trap and reflect light, that gives *The Burghers* their vitality and hence their meaning. What emerges is not Rodin's technical skill, but his compassionate understanding of the human condition.

128

In his final plan for *The Burghers* Rodin eliminated the pedestal and placed the group at ground level. In so doing he ran the risk of losing the impact of distance and apparent size, for the figures are only slightly more than six feet tall and stand on a base less than a foot high. But by exaggerating the hands and feet and by using unusually expressive gestures, Rodin gave each figure the illusion of compelling stature. The burgher above clutches his head in an agony of fear: he stands momentarily tormented, his robe twisted around his body, and by this device Rodin helps to move the viewer around the group. As seen at right, the robes are parted and thickly muscled legs and sturdy feet show through. In a complex harmony of forms the legs seem to step solidly forward—another subtle reminder by Rodin of the collective resolution of the burghers.

Sketch for *Monument to Victor Hugo*, plaster, c. 1890

Rodin's failure to create a successful memorial to the great Victor Hugo is perhaps understandable. He had come to think of Hugo, whom he had also sculpted in life, as a "French Jupiter," a titan of literature. Impressed also with the novelist's noble self-exile on the isle of Guernsey in protest against the regime of Napoleon III, Rodin loaded his monument with literary, mythological and biographical references that finally overwhelmed it. In the plaster study above, Hugo reclines pensively on a rock—representing Guernsey —with one outstretched arm (since broken) quieting the waves while nude muses flutter about. In another study *(right)*, Rodin placed Hugo on a rocky ledge while sea sirens beckon him from below and Iris, messenger of the gods, flies overhead. Pompous and awkward, both monuments—and other versions that Rodin offered —were rejected as unsuitable to the proposed site outside the dignified Panthéon in Paris.

Sketch for *Monument to Victor Hugo*, bronze, c. 1893

Balzac was a prodigious lover, a reckless speculator and art collector, an unabashed social climber, and, above all, France's greatest novelist. Unloved in childhood, misunderstood and unappreciated in youth, saddled with crushing debts all his life, he carved out a phenomenal career as a writer by exploiting his unusual gifts of observation and imagination and by his exceptional capacity for work—16 hours a day for weeks on end was not uncommon. After turning out dozens of potboilers under pseudonyms, Balzac began to write the novels that he eventually organized into a stupendous series, *La Comédie Humaine*, a panorama of French life across all levels of society. Peopled with more than 2,000 characters, the 90-odd books and stories that he completed still left him some 50 novels short of his goal. But by 1850 his exhausting work habits had cost him his eyesight and his vigor and he died, only 51.

A monument to Balzac had been planned since the day after his funeral—at which Victor Hugo delivered the eulogy—but by 1891 it was still unrealized. That year the Société des Gens de Lettres, an association of authors, commissioned Rodin to create a Balzac memorial. Tremendously challenged by the prospect, he made scores of studies: heads of the mature Balzac, including the forceful terra cotta at right, and full-length figures, both nude and clothed, including those on the following pages. Gradually, Rodin evolved his final conception. He wrote the Society that he planned more than a likeness, that he hoped to express Balzac's "relentless labor . . . the difficulties of his life . . . his ceaseless struggle . . . and magnificent courage." He showed Balzac's leonine head, with its deeply gouged features, rising above a solid body cloaked in a voluminous robe. Rilke, the German poet who was Rodin's secretary for a time, believed that the sculptor had captured "creation's pride, arrogance, ecstasy, intoxication."

Both the Société des Gens de Lettres and the public thought otherwise, however, when the *Balzac* was exhibited in 1898. Rather than try to convert those who saw the work as a sheer monstrosity, Rodin repaid the money advanced him and withdrew the sculpture to the privacy of his garden at Meudon. In 1939 it was finally cast in bronze and erected in Paris. As Rodin had predicted some 40 years earlier, his *Balzac* had made its way alone.

Study of Balzac nude, 1893-1895

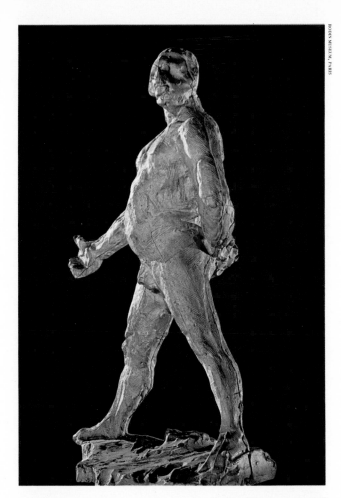

Study of Balzac nude, 1893

Study of Balzac in frock coat, 1892-1895

Study of Balzac in dressing gown, 1895-1897

Balzac, bronze, 1897

VI

The World's Foremost Sculptor

Far from doing Rodin's reputation any harm, the *Balzac* affair greatly enhanced it. All across Europe newspapers reported on the uproar caused in the art capital of the world by one man and one statue. To readers who had hitherto known of Rodin only as a Parisian given to highly erotic forms, he now seemed an archcrusader against conservatism, a standard-bearer of the new. The day of his international fame was at hand.

The spreading interest in him was not solely of the *Balzac's* making. From the mid-1890s on, his work was seen with increasing frequency at exhibitions beyond the borders of France, in such cities as Dusseldorf, Vienna, Prague, Stockholm and Geneva. His reception was not always wholehearted; the Musée Rath in Geneva acquired his contorted *Crouching Woman* only to have second thoughts and secrete it in a basement as improper, just as the Chicago World's Fair had tucked away *The Kiss*. But in general the times were propitious for the unusual. To many minds the approaching turn of the century conveyed the idea of a watershed, of an end and a beginning, and there was a restive sense that time had run out on old ideas and tastes. Among the dynamic new movements in art were the sinuous *art nouveau* of France, the *Jugendstil* (style of youth) of Germany and the rebellious *Sezession* (secession) group in staid Austria. Collectors of paintings and drawings were beginning to relish the sardonic bite of Toulouse-Lautrec and the macabre expressionism of the Norwegian Edvard Munch. As he entered his sixties Rodin, veteran of the past, found himself identified with the future.

In 1899, the year after the climactic collision over the *Balzac*, exhibitions of Rodin's work were shown in Brussels and Rotterdam, drawing large crowds, especially when the master himself put in an appearance. Their brilliant success in terms of attendance, and the tangible rewards in terms of sales and commissions, not only restored his ego after years of tribulations with committees and juries, but enlarged it. He now hit upon an astonishing scheme. The French state, always alert to centennials, planned to mount another Universal Exposition in 1900 to herald the arrival of the new century. This time, Rodin resolved, he would not be just another exhibitor as he had been at the Exposition of

1889, subject to the vagaries of committees in accepting and placing his entries. If there were so many people who wanted to see and even buy his work, he would erect his own independent pavilion, at his own cost, for an *Exposition Rodin* just outside the fairgrounds.

This daring idea seems to have been his alone, although it may have been inspired by a similar step taken by the great painter of realism Gustave Courbet in 1855. Unlike other artists of his day, Rodin had no personal agent or dealer at his side. Cézanne, for instance, had found in Ambroise Vollard a diligent advocate who had put on the painter's first one-man show in 1895, when Cézanne was well into middle age. Young Pablo Picasso, arriving in Paris in the centennial year to embark upon his career, was later to have the equally brilliant help of Daniel-Henry Kahnweiler in pushing him. But Rodin, flinty of purpose and as sharp with money as a Norman trader, chose to promote himself. He took little advice and split no fees. Whenever exhibits of his works were wanted here or there, he selected and assembled them himself at the country estate he had recently acquired at Meudon or in his Rue de l'Université studio, setting his own terms, preferring to sell directly from the source.

In planning his exposition he proved himself both a master salesman and psychologist of the public. First he tested his pulling power in Holland and Belgium, not only by making personal appearances but by sending young Judith Cladel to scout and report reactions to his works and even to lecture on "the truth about sculpture." Initially, the idea of lecturing frightened her, but Rodin assured her that the public "would much rather hear a young woman's accurate and straightforward explanation than some well-known man's high-sounding oration that did not get to the root of the thing," and he proceeded to indoctrinate her in the principles of his art. (The precise nature of his personal relations with the comely Judith, 33 years his junior, remains a subject of speculation, but it appears that although he was still voracious for almost any woman who came within his reach, in this case he preserved a fatherly attitude; Judith, for her part, would one day write about his affairs with dispassion.)

Her reports from along the way helped confirm Rodin in his intentions for 1900. He balanced all the work he had to show against what it might cost to show it and decided to take the risk: in any event an *Exposition Rodin* was bound to be a sensation. All he had in hand was a personal "reserve," as he called it, of 20,000 francs. He persuaded three Paris bankers, Louis Dorizon, Johanny Peytal and Albert Kahn, to advance him 20,000 francs each; with this money, and with the permission of the municipal authorities, he set about building his pavilion on the Place de l'Alma near the gates to the fairgrounds. The building was well over 200 feet long and more than 40 feet high, with a glass roof and 16 tall windows.

Inside Rodin placed the better part of the work of a lifetime—more than 150 sculptures large and small, a score or more of paintings and a sampling of drawings. All his best-known figures were there, from *The Man with the Broken Nose* to *The Burghers of Calais, The Kiss, The Thinker, The Prodigal* and onward to *Balzac*. Also included were a skeleton version of *The Gates of Hell*, minus many figures on which Rodin was still working, and his *Ascendancy*, in which a female bestrides her male in the act of sex (to which the police made no objection). Among other more recent figures on display, wrought in intervals during Rodin's struggles with the *Balzac*, were a *Faun Abducting a Woman* and a *Hand of God*, in which a huge palm rising out of primeval stone molds and holds Adam and Eve.

Rodin knew that so huge a venture would break him if it did not succeed. Added to the expense of putting up the pavilion, he faced the costs of haulage, of installation, of maintaining and protecting the exhibits, and of preparing bronze or marble versions of certain selected figures. Ultimately his indebtedness reached 150,000 francs—an immense sum to try to recoup from door receipts and on-the-spot sales. To forestall possible financial disaster, he organized a promotion campaign that drew on all his leading supporters in the art world. The portraitist and etcher Eugène Carrière designed posters for the show that proclaimed the price of admission—weekdays one franc, Fridays (the "select" day for gallery-going) five francs. An illustrated catalogue arranged for by Rodin was prefaced by tributes from four prominent artists of diverse tastes—including Monet, who wrote: "I . . . set down my great admiration for the man, unique in his time and great among the greatest." Rodin got the French Minister of Education, Georges Leygues, to preside at the opening of the exhibition. A public dinner was held in his honor at which more than 100 artistic and literary lights were present, including Toulouse-Lautrec and Oscar Wilde, who thought Rodin "by far the greatest poet in France." Offering the toast to Rodin, the critic Karl Boës hailed him as an artist who prevented "tired nations from despairing of themselves." Rodin replied with a toast to Youth.

This was not all. The cultural review *La Plume*, sponsor of the dinner, issued a book-length symposium of accolades by 21 critics. Rodin, with an eye to the gate receipts at his pavilion, arranged for lectures there by some of the testimonial writers about the merits of his work. The results surpassed his wildest hopes. Although the attendance figures were disappointing—there were wits who referred to the exhibit as "the Rodin desert"—this was amply offset by the prestige of many of the visitors and the fact that those who came also bought. Soon a jubilant Rodin was able to write a friend, "I have sold 200,000 francs' worth, and I hope a little more. There are further orders too. Almost all the museums have bought from me: Philadelphia, *The Thinker*; Copenhagen, 80,000 francs for a separate room of my own in the museum; Hamburg, Dresden, Budapest, etc."

With orders pouring in, his problem now was to keep up with the demand. Most of the orders were commissions not so much for new works as for bronze casts or marble replicas of works already on exhibit. In a sense these were requests for duplicates, but Rodin's more sophisticated patrons knew that they could justly call their acquisitions "originals." Bronze casts, although derived from a single plaster model by mechanical means, can still differ from one another by variations in the seams and in the nature of the patina placed upon the metal. Marble replicas show

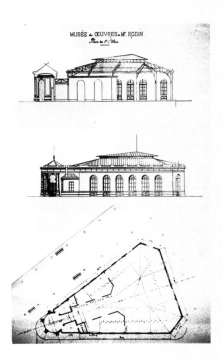

The architectural plans above were for the pavilion Rodin built to house his one-man show near the Paris Exposition of 1900. A simple, functional building with huge windows and a glass roof, it contained a large hall partitioned by pale yellow drapes. The effect, one visitor noted, was that of "an abode of light." To advertise the show, the sculptor's friend Eugène Carrière designed the poster below, depicting Rodin caressing a treelike shape. Carrière believed that Rodin was beholden to organic forms, and expounded this idea in a laudatory article for the exhibition catalogue.

even greater variations; often they differ in size, and they may reflect a further realization of the artist's basic idea, since he can put his individual impress on each replica. Just how many casts or replicas ought to be made, once there is demand for them, is the question the artist alone can decide; bronze casts, in particular, cannot be turned out indefinitely without some loss in quality. The number to be made is essentially a matter for the sculptor's esthetic—and ethical—sense to determine.

Rodin, dazzled by the prices he was offered, often yielded to the lure of selling multiple facsimiles. In the case of *The Man with the Broken Nose*, which was growing all the more popular, he allowed at least 10 bronze casts of it to be made for clients in England alone. Yet whether bronze or marble was called for, he did seek to control the quality of the work of transference out of plaster, employing highly skilled artists and technicians to mold and to cast, to cut, finish and polish stone, while he moved among them indicating corrections or occasionally taking up a cutting tool to make some final improvement. At any given time after 1900 a dozen or more assistants might be found working for him: Antoine Bourdelle, the chief marble carver; another young French sculptor, Charles Despiau; the American student Malvina Hoffman, one day to win her own niche in the world of sculpture; and, among others, a professional finisher who bore the haunting name of Seraphin Soudbidine. Some of them labored in the Rue de l'Université studio, others out at the Rodin retreat in Meudon, which he now converted into a headquarters for intensive production.

The pavilion he had created to house the *Exposition Rodin* proved an unexpected boon. After the show closed, Rodin had the building disassembled, carted out to his country seat and re-erected there as an immense workshop. When not engaged on immediate orders, his assistants and students were encouraged (as Camille Claudel had been, in her day) to provide him with clay models of human hands, legs or feet that might fit in when some variant of a figure was called for. In 1901, riding the crest of demand, Rodin allowed his name to be used to start L'Académie Rodin on the Boulevard Montparnasse, where regular art courses were given. And a workshop nearby was devoted to the dissemination of marble versions of his works, produced by his disciples Bourdelle and Despiau. Unquestionably a "Rodin factory" was in the making, with some distant echoes of Carrier-Belleuse' mass production.

It sometimes seemed that success was going to Rodin's head, but understandably so. Once unleashed, the interest in him appeared to be limitless. Europeans reacted to him as if they had seen no other sculptor worthy of the name in his lifetime—which, one could argue, was the truth. In London a public subscription paid for the purchase of his *St. John* for the South Kensington Museum, and a private donor presented a cast of *The Thinker* to the nation. When Rodin arrived from Paris in 1902 to respond to these honors, a public banquet was staged for him at the Café Royal. A member of the Cabinet, George Wyndham, presided, and the occasion ended with the kind of demonstration usually reserved for opera divas after an evening of special triumph: art students

Rodin enjoyed taking visitors through his studio at Meudon. In this joshing illustration from a German magazine, Rodin—swathed in a voluminous dressing gown, as he had depicted his *Balzac*—conducts a tour of his high-ceilinged, unheated gallery. His guests are four members of the British Parliament; the year is 1907, when the sculptor received an honorary degree from Oxford.

from the South Kensington and Slade schools unhitched the horses of Rodin's carriage and drew it themselves, while a visiting American painter named John Singer Sargent held the reins. That same year the ancient city of Prague bought Rodin's *Age of Bronze* and received him with ovations; he responded by giving it a cast of one of his burghers of Calais. In London again the next year, he was elected president of the International Society of Painters, Sculptors and Engravers, upon the death of its founder, James McNeill Whistler. Still the honors came: his own government promoted Rodin to the third-highest rank of the Legion of Honor, that of Commander, and in 1905 *The Thinker*—this time enlarged to heroic size—was installed in Paris in front of the Panthéon, the costs defrayed by a public subscription of 15,000 francs.

Meanwhile Rodin's prestige as a portrait sculptor had so skyrocketed that he raised his price for elite sitters to a phenomenal 40,000 francs per head. From Chicago the dazzlingly bejeweled Mrs. Potter Palmer, the department-store heiress and owner of the Palmer House (its barbershop floor inlaid with silver dollars), arrived in Paris to be "done" by Rodin. From England such socialite beauties as the Countess of Warwick, Lady Sackville-West and Miss Eve Fairfax came to sit; from Germany came the exquisitely cultivated Countess Helene von Nostitz (nee Hindenburg). Doubtless Rodin did not charge her his going price, since at the moment he was having an affair with her.

Though he enjoyed sculpting lovely women, when 40,000 francs were involved he was ready to lay aside other work and sculpt men of substance too. He turned out a series of busts of American magnates, among them the newspaper publisher Joseph Pulitzer, the railroad baron E. H. Harriman and the financier Thomas Fortune Ryan; the results were sturdy, hard-faced portraits that enhanced Rodin's pocketbook more than his artistic name. Far more winning was a head he made in 1903 of his English friend George Wyndham, then Secretary of State for Ireland—a subtle study of a pensive, sensitive man turned 40. Even more striking was the head he made in 1906 of George Bernard Shaw, for which the fee was negotiated between the wealthy but prudent Mrs. Shaw and Rodin's secretary. The secretary involved was the young German poet Rainer Maria Rilke, an ardent admirer who had attached himself to Rodin's household.

Once Rodin accepted a commission, he was not a man to give his client hurried treatment, even if other business pressed upon him. He first received Shaw—world-famous at 50 as author, critic and socialist spokesman—at the Rue de l'Université studio, then invited him to journey out to Meudon daily over a period of a month for prolonged sittings. Shaw agreed, himself dropping other work. Rodin spoke no English and confessed he had not read a word of Shaw. Shaw, however, spoke passable French, and in due time a warm association developed as they studied each other in the studio overlooking the Seine.

Rilke watched the making of Shaw's bust with utter fascination. "I was present at the first sittings," he wrote, "and saw for the first time how Rodin tackles his work. First there is a firmly shaped clay dummy, consisting of nothing but a ball set on something that supports it like a shoulder. . . . He begins his work by first placing his model at a very short distance, about half a step from the stand. With a big iron compass he took the measurement from the top of the head to the tip of the beard. . . . After he had further cut out the eye sockets very quickly, so that something like a nose was formed, and had marked the place for the mouth with an indentation such as children might make for a snowman, he began, with his model standing very close, to make first four profiles, then eight, then sixteen. . . . Yesterday, at the third session, he seated Shaw in a cunning little child's armchair (that ironic and by no means uncongenial scoffer was greatly entertained by this) and cut off the head of the bust with a wire (Shaw, whom the bust already remarkably resembled, in a superior sort of way watched this decapitation with indescribable joy) and worked on the recumbent head. . . . Then it was set on again."

That was as Rilke saw it, sitting beside two geniuses, one at work, the other at palaver. Shaw himself, as he remembered the occasion, was not full of "indescribable joy." He thought Rodin's method of evolving the modeled head somewhat odd, and felt that Rodin was going through virtually the whole history of sculpture while doing so. Recalling the experience in an article long afterward, Shaw wrote that "within the space of a month my bust passed successively, under my eyes, through all the stages of art's evolution. The first fifteen minutes having passed, he became serious and began a careful reproduction of my features in their exact dimensions of life. Then, this representation went back mysteriously to the cradle of Christian art and, at this moment, I had the desire to say again: For the love of heaven, stop and give me that. It is truly a Byzantine masterpiece. Then, little by little it seemed that Bernini intermingled with the work. Then, to my great horror the bust softened in order to become a commendable eighteenth-century morceau, elegant enough to make one believe that Houdon had retouched a head by Canova or Thorvaldsen. . . . Once again, a century rolled by in a single night, and the bust became a bust by Rodin and it was the living reproduction of the head that reposes on my shoulders. It was a process that seemed to belong to the study of an embryologist and not to an artist."

At one point Mrs. Shaw arrived on the scene and complicated matters by suggesting to Rodin that artists had a way of drawing her husband's reputation, rather than the man himself. Rodin replied stiffly: "I know nothing of Monsieur Shaw's reputation; but what there is there I will give you." Later he told a friend: "Shaw does not speak French well; but he expresses himself with such violence that he imposes himself." Still, sculptor and subject got along famously at the luncheons that followed the sittings, Shaw with his vegetarian diet and water, Rodin tucking in napkin for his sturdy repast of meat and his carafe of wine. The head Rodin finally brought forth was all amiability coupled with shrewd intellect—a sharp-witted exploration of a man whose wit he could not quite understand. Over the years the two corresponded with expressions of mutual esteem. On one occasion, when Rodin asked Shaw's permission to make several copies of the bust, Shaw answered,

"Cher maître, please have as many copies cast as you wish; the work is yours; mine is the honor. I am always proud to be known as your model. You are the only man in whose presence I feel really humble." Humility—from Shaw!

With the comings and goings of clients and the bustle of assistants and secretaries, life at Meudon took on a manorial atmosphere. Rodin's income from portrait commissions alone was running to perhaps 200,000 francs a year—this in addition to earnings from the sale of replicas of existing works, bought as far away as Tokyo. The complex establishment that had formed around him called for a fitting setting for the master. He now developed his Meudon property into a show place, although in a fashion quite his own.

The country home he had bought in the 1890s, some miles downriver from Paris on several acres, was anything but pretentious. It contained only a narrow brick villa, high-gabled in the style of the period of Louis XIII. Downstairs the house had a small salon and a dining room that could comfortably seat no more than eight; upstairs there were two bedrooms. The beauty of the property lay in its location. It was high on a bluff a few kilometers by carriage from the Meudon railway station and was approached by a long avenue of chestnut trees above a great bend of the Seine; its orchards and hedges dropped down to give a plunging view into the valley—Sèvres nearby, the woods of Saint-Cloud next, the towers of Paris itself in the distance. Rodin did little to make the house, known as the Villa des Brillants, more comfortable. He had its rooms brightly painted, but there were no rugs, no easy chairs or sofas, only stiff-backed side chairs made of cane. The gaunt old house on the wind-swept bluff remained unheated save by a few porcelain corner ovens; in winter months Rodin wore a velvet beret and rolls of woolen scarves indoors.

Despite its discomforts the Villa des Brillants in time began to live up to its name. Well off at last, able to indulge himself as a collector, Rodin filled it with art objects from near and far—paintings and draw-

At left is the home Rodin bought in the Parisian suburb of Meudon in 1897, after his doctor suggested he move to a more restful environment. A modest estate, it had nevertheless inspired its previous owner, a lady painter, to give it the romantic name of Villa des Brillants (Diamond Villa), presumably for the night glitter of lights along the nearby Seine. Beyond the house is the pavilion Rodin built for his one-man show in Paris in 1900 and later disassembled and re-erected at his retreat. By 1908 he was ready to return to city life, and rented the ground floor of an 18th Century town house (above), the Hôtel Biron, which stood in a lovely, tree-filled private park in the heart of Paris.

147

ings by his friend Monet, Attic vases, Roman heads and Egyptian fragments picked up from Paris dealers. In effect he planned a small museum, with cabinets of examples of his own work along the walls also. Outside, Rodin's innovations were even more striking. At his direction copses, grottoes, pools, walks and crosswalks came into being, ornamented by his own sculpture or examples from classic times (he was particularly proud of a Roman replica of a satyr by the great Greek sculptor Praxiteles). The resurrected pavilion of the *Exposition Rodin* was installed near the house. Rodin also bought an entire façade of a 17th Century French mansion that was about to be torn down, the Château d'Issy, and erected it in his garden. Meanwhile, in the yards that grew flowers, fruits and vegetables, outbuildings were refurbished, and one of these was tenanted by Rilke in 1905 and 1906 in his capacity as Rodin's secretary and factotum.

Rilke, then turning 30, was one of the most remarkable literary personalities to emerge from Central Europe, and his intimacy with Rodin —who knew no German, though Rilke spoke fair French—is a story unto itself. Born in Prague, educated at German universities, a man of exquisite sensitivity, Rilke was gaining a name as the leading modern poet in the German language next to his contemporary Stefan George. He was also a teller of tales in parables and an indefatigable seeker of inspirational companionship—a mystic of sorts, a would-be disciple of great men from whom he sensed an emanation. He had made a pilgrimage to Russia to Leo Tolstoi at his home at Yasnaya Polyana. Next he turned to Rodin, in whom he felt some mighty power also, and arrived in Paris in 1902 with a commission from a German publisher to write a monograph about the man and his work.

Rodin received Rilke more cordially than Tolstoi had and invited him to Meudon, where the poet soon lapsed into a state of adulation. "To me," he exclaimed to Rodin, "your work is the voice I harken amid the silence that surrounds me, the dawn and twilight of all my days and the sky of my nights." Lengthy interviews as they walked under the chestnut trees or among the sculptures resulted in a searching if somewhat rapturous published study by Rilke that dwelt upon Rodin's "deep harmony with nature" and the "intuitive quality" of each of his portraits ("each face that he has modeled he has lifted out of the bondage of the present into the freedom of the future"). Rodin was moved by so ardent, perceptive and eloquent an interpreter and in 1905 invited him to join the Villa des Brillants household. Rilke felt that he had found his mecca.

To be sure, life at the Villa had its complications. Always there was the problem of Rose, now far out of her depth amid its growing celebrity. Manifestly she was incapable of receiving guests or playing hostess at table. Rilke recalled that on his first visit to Meudon no one at dinner was introduced to anyone else, and that when Rodin complained of the lateness of the meal, Rose roused herself from lethargy only to snap that he should have blamed the cook, then proceeded confusedly to shove dishes about the table—"a sad scene," Rilke commented. On another occasion, when the guest of honor was a high government official, she appeared in so garish a red gown that she was sent upstairs to change. On yet another day, when the Japanese Ambassador to France arrived to a flower-strewn welcome, he asked to meet the lady of the house; Rose was finally produced from the kitchen, hands swollen from washing dishes. Often, when guests were present, Rodin would not allow her to appear at all.

Still, she was the chatelaine, and there were moments when she must have derived a wry satisfaction from her role. Sometimes, at nightfall, a wraithlike presence prowled around the garden, hiding in the bushes to pry at Rodin and Rose. The specter was that of Camille Claudel, forlorn, mentally disturbed and compelled to revisit or at least haunt her old lover. Rose would shout curses at her when she caught sight of her in the shadows.

Whether Rodin was moved by the apparition is not recorded. Camille's love had been supplanted by the admiration of distinguished visitors. Grown expansive and loquacious with the years, Rodin captivated his guests with his table talk. He might discourse on the relative merits of various Gothic cathedrals or of the 18th Century novels of Henry Fielding as against those of Samuel Richardson. At his behest his secretaries had begun to take down much of his talk in the form of notes: he was planning to publish his ideas on art. Judith Cladel, who was often in residence as companion and assistant, played the piano for him after dinner. In the minuscule court over which he reigned, his relations with Judith, at least, remained unruffled. Not so with his male secretaries. Rilke was but one of a long succession of them, all men of intelligence and artistic bent who frequently felt the blast of Rodin's heightening temperament and temper and who periodically rose and fell from his favor.

He was reaching the age of crotchets. Although he was a poor letter writer himself, a passion for paper work seized him, and he insisted on amassing huge boxed files of correspondence, estimates, invoices, receipts, drafts and redrafts— a *"monstre paperassier,"* secretary Anthony Ludovici called him, likening him to a document-obsessed bureaucrat. (The high-spirited Ludovici did not endear himself to Rodin when he persisted in addressing him simply as "Monsieur" instead of the more respectful *"maître."*) Suspicions that his secretaries were not serving him adequately, or were going behind his back, began to prey on Rodin. There were storms and accusations, which on occasion Rose herself tried to stem, pointing out to the secretaries that she, too, had been accused of neglect. Rilke fell victim to one of Rodin's outbreaks after just six months at Meudon and was abruptly dismissed.

The slender, earnest poet-acolyte had taken on all manner of duties. Although his own French was imperfect, he had handled Rodin's voluminous correspondence, writing responses for his signature. He had also struggled with accounts. When fired on the grounds that he had been in communication with friends of Rodin without his knowledge, Rilke wrote a letter from Paris that may well have startled Rodin, since it expressed unwavering, lasting devotion: "Here I am, banished like a thief from the little house you so generously installed me in. I am deeply wounded, but I understand. . . . I shall not see you again, but for me, as for the Apostles who stay behind, saddened, forlorn, life is beginning afresh—a life which will celebrate your lofty example and find in you its consolation, justification, and strength."

There was a clear and present danger, amid the adulation and awards and self-indulgence of his sixties, that Rodin might become a prisoner of his fame. Yet he managed, at least in part, to resist this. His still-alert energies and urge for originality kept breaking through. Keeping up with portrait commissions and managing his art collection consumed the major part of his time; yet he reserved enough of it to pursue numerous new artistic ventures for his own pleasure. They represented a distinct departure from his own recent past. The day of his highly charged, strident and monumental sculpture was done. After about 1900 he abandoned bold and battered forms such as those on *The Gates* or the *Balzac* and turned to serene figures, most of them small and intimate, or to gently evocative efforts such as *The Cathedral*—a pair of symbolic hands raised in prayer. These, without question, were works of reconciliation, of Rodin seeking to make his peace with the world.

He had long felt in himself what he called an "oscillation"—an alternating attraction to two contrasting founts in art. One was Michelangelo, and what Rodin saw as the great Florentine's "condensed passion" and perception of tragedy. The other was provided by the classic Greeks, best exemplified by Phidias, with his "tranquil charm" and air of "contentment, calm, grace, balance." But now Rodin had made a choice: in his own words, he had "returned to the antique"—meaning the antique style of the gentle Phidias rather than that of the sculptors of the stark Archaic period or of the turbulent Hellenistic period. Rodin found that he was no longer attuned to Michelangelo's austerity and mistrust of life; serenity, he declared, was now his goal: "Earthly activity, imperfect as it may be, is still beautiful and good." The causes of this change in him were no doubt mixed: worldly success, the sense of battles fought and won, the autumnal quieting of fires after the summer's heat, all played their part.

There was another significant change in Rodin's approach to sculpture at this time. In earlier years he had seldom tackled the tedious process of translating his efforts into marble. Now, however, he began to prefer working with marble in mind rather than with bronze—exquisitely smooth and polished marbles, finished for him by Bourdelle and other assistants. He spoke of pursuing simplicity and harmony; he also yielded to a certain softness both of subject and treatment. Unlike the lofty resignation of Beethoven's last quartets, or the mighty reaffirmation of life in his final symphony, the mood of Rodin's later sculptures tended to be affirmative but bland. He produced a lovely *Muse*, rising out of the stone; there were numerous nymphs and satyrs, made with a lifetime's accumulated skill, yet somewhat insubstantial after what he had done before; there was *The Secret*, a study of tender hands enclosing some undefinable talisman; and there was *Beside the Sea*, a distinctly sentimental figure of a maiden on the strand who might have come out of Watteau—or out of Carrier-Belleuse.

Such works helped reassure established clients: Rodin had evidently reached his limits, and would not go "too far." Still, he was capable of surprises. One was his new-found absorption with the dance, which together with his longtime interest in Oriental art gave a new turn to his sexagenarian years. In the first decade of the 20th Century all Europe was obsessed by an interest in the exotic. Especially in Paris, Japanese prints and East Indian figurines, as well as imported Cambodian and Javanese dancers, were the rage. In their joyous movements Rodin found an enlivening departure, particularly now that he was no longer burdened with tragic thoughts of the fate of man. He was also enormously stimulated by the works of Japanese artists, those extraordinary simplifiers who could enclose a whole figure with just a few pen strokes, as if spontaneously; Rodin had long been an apostle of improvisation, of the lightning-quick sketch. Another fascination lay in the bounding little figures of Indonesian dancers, seen both in the flesh and in the prancing silhouettes of them being sold in Paris. He struck off his own clay models of them, often hardly larger than a hand.

And what could be more spontaneous, in Rodin's view, than the "modern" dance of the West itself, or more ravishing? Here was Loie Fuller from America, performing with her wands and veils at the 1900 Universal Exposition and at the Folies-Bergère, and here was Isadora Duncan, also from America, a far greater artist, proclaiming a revolution in freedom for the human body. Isadora proved the ideal subject for Rodin. His eyes never off her dancing figure, he would dash off almost instantaneous paper sketches of her, a whirl of pen or pencil here, a wash thrown on there. Sculpture might be his first love, but his final masterworks are to be found among these sketches.

Loie Fuller, pursued by hosts of admirers, became and remained a Rodin friend. So did Isadora, after the initial encounter with him which did not quite come off—that "pilgrimage" to his studio, which, as she described it in her flowery way, was that of "Psyche seeking the God Pan in his grotto, only I was not seeking the way to Eros, but only to Apollo." Left intact after his hot-breathed advances, she soon came out to dance barefoot on the grass at a *fête champêtre* near Meudon and soon also opened a school on the opposite bank of the Seine at Bellevue. Rodin came there to draw both her and her fledglings, sighing that he would have loved to have had such models when he was young.

Both professionally and personally, woman still preoccupied him. For a while he left Meudon for an idyll in Italy with the charming Countess Helene von Nostitz. At her villa on the Ligurian Sea, under the supposed chaperonage of her mother, she introduced Rodin to Goethe's *Faust*. There were intimate walks on the beach and evenings of Beethoven; the Countess found Rodin so engrossing that she wrote a small book about her seaside and twilight conversations with him—in which, however, she did most of the talking.

Everyone who was anyone, it seemed, wanted to meet Rodin, talk with him, even perform for him. In 1905 Wanda Landowska had her harpsichord sent out to the Villa des Brillants to play for him. He received her in a Prince Albert, with white beard flowing, as he did

Illinois-born Loie Fuller *(above)* graduated from American burlesque to the Folies Bergère, where her serpentine "skirt dance" made her the toast of Paris. Dressed in voluminous shimmering silk costumes, and waving wands hung with huge veils, "La Loïe" whirled and twirled in imitation of moths and flames. So popular was her dance that it inspired the *art nouveau* bronze lamp below, in which the sculptor gallantly slimmed down her pudgy figure.

151

HIGH LIFE AT MEUDON

The famous, the talented and the beautiful flocked to Rodin's country seat at Meudon to meet him, perform for him or, if they were rich enough to afford his prices, to pose for him. After the success of his one-man exposition in 1900, the flood of visitors swelled to include members of international society. Since they had bought heavily at the show —and thus helped defray the cost of the exhibition pavilion—Rodin warmly welcomed them. He could be a gracious host even when the arrivals disrupted his working schedule. The guests he found most congenial, however, were artistic personalities, and when they were female as well his pleasure was doubled. This album of photographs shows Rodin, secure in his success, at ease amid his acres and basking in the company of some of the most gifted and exciting women of his time.

With dancer Loie Fuller (left) and R

With the Duchesse de Choiseul.

With his biographer, Judith Cle

Eleanora Duse. Wearing a colossal plumed hat, the great actress recited from the French classics for Rodin. Another notable who could not make it to Meudon, the King of Greece, invited Rodin to make a sea voyage to Athens. Rodin demurred, fearing *mal de mer:* a Channel crossing was enough of a venture for him in that respect. He was always ready to risk that body of water for more honors. In 1907 he crossed over to receive a doctorate at Oxford; the other recipients that year were Mark Twain, the composer Camille Saint-Saëns and General William Booth of the Salvation Army. Rodin returned home with the scarlet academic robe he had worn at the ceremony and proudly sport-

With harpsichordist Wanda Landowska.

With actress Eleanora Duse and a Cabinet Minister.

With Isadora Duncan (seated left foreground), Rose (at Rodin's left) and anonymous admirers.

ed it in the garden at Meudon. He did so only once, however, abandoning the idea after he saw Judith Cladel struggle to conceal her smile at what she called his "toga." But he did continue to wear the flopping black velvet cap that had been part of his investiture costume—a piece of headgear that lent him a look reminiscent of the elderly Rembrandt.

Rodin's studio in Paris was also a magnet for visitors. One was the Countess Elisabeth Greffuhle, the supreme society beauty of the decade and center of its most dashing set. In due course she was portrayed as the Duchess of Guermantes in Marcel Proust's masterwork, *Remembrance of Things Past*; why Rodin himself, with his eye for beauty, did

PLEASURES OF PROSPERITY

"I have always lived like a working man," Rodin liked to say, but the routine he followed at Meudon had little semblance of the proletarian. When there was no press of visitors to cope with, he spent much time with the foreman of the estate arranging his acquisitions of antique art in the private museum he was assembling. At midday he would return to the house or, in good weather, go to the garden to eat the meal that Rose prepared and served him. It was only in Rodin's workshop at Meudon, staffed by assistants whose work he supervised, that traces of his earlier habits remained. As one art critic wrote, "Nothing in Rodin's surroundings resembles the society studios of fashionable sculptors . . . everything reminds one of the craftsman, wearing wooden shoes with dust and smears of clay on his garments."

With his foreman, Rose and his dogs.

Posing in his Oxford gown, with a lady journalist, a young friend and Rose.

Lunch in the garden with Rose.

not portray her is puzzling, except that he knew of her difficult ways with sculptors—when Alexandre Falguière sculpted her, she disliked the head and threw it out, keeping only the shoulders. There was more sedate company for Rodin at the Élysée Palace, home of the President of the Republic. Frequently invited for banquets, he would appear with his white mane beautifully coifed and curled, his person sprinkled with eau de cologne and his stiff white shirt front festooned with medals.

But Rodin was happiest as host. A climactic day arrived in 1908 when no less a personage than King Edward VII of England coached out to Meudon to visit him and view his work. Rodin had arranged a spe-

cial exhibition in his immense studio-gallery, grouping figures around the central showpiece, *The Kiss.* The reception went off handsomely (Rose stayed out of sight) and Rodin was commissioned to make a bust —not of Edward himself, but of one of his special lady favorites of the time. The assignment must have particularly intrigued Rodin, for at the moment he was at work on a bust of his own newest favorite, the successor to Countess von Nostitz, and a woman of even loftier title, the Duchesse de Choiseul. Born Claire Coudert of New York, Rodin's duchess was rich, wildly amorous, demanding and alcoholic, and she was destined to unsettle the peace he sought in his advancing years.

An Affair with the Dance

Rodin once told an inquiring friend that the first law in his code of art was "Movement is the soul of all things." He was fascinated by every aspect of movement in nature, and especially by the movement of the human body. Yet, surprisingly, he showed little interest in the dance until he reached his sixties. Then, entering a sunny period after the storms of his earlier years, he turned to the study of dancers in action as a new phase in his never-ending exploration of movement. Young Cambodian dancers, the Russian Vaslav Nijinsky and the American Isadora Duncan—he was charmed by them all. And he responded with many small sculptural studies and hundreds of dazzling intimate drawings.

His drawing technique required special virtuosity: he would trace an outline, often with one unbroken stroke of his pencil, without taking his eyes off the model. Sketch after sketch slipped from his pad to the floor as he hurried to catch each transient gesture. Later, to give the figure volume, he would fill in the outlines with a brushful of watercolor. He relied on what he called his "sincere observation" to enable him to "pass over useless details and seize only upon the truth of the whole."

To Rodin, this truth lay in expressing the language of movement, a language that could be universally understood and used to help man come to know himself. As he put it: "I have always tried to express the inner feelings by the mobility of the muscles."

Rodin wrote, "It is a false idea that drawing in itself can be beautiful. It is only beautiful through the truths and feelings it translates." In this study of a long-legged dancer—sometimes identified as Isadora Duncan—lightly springing through space, he conveyed a vivid feeling of *joie de vivre*.

Dancer, c. 1901

Cambodian Dancer, 1906

161

In the spring of 1912 Vaslav Nijinsky first performed his ballet *The Afternoon of a Faun* before a flabbergasted Paris audience. The ballet dealt with the awakening of sexual instincts, and though Nijinsky tried to give the story a mythic quality by making his hero half-man, half-

animal and setting the action in classical Greece, the sensuality of the dancing was more than most balletomanes were ready for: they called the production scandalous. Rodin was among an enthusiastic minority at the première that acclaimed the new work for its

162

honesty, and he asked Nijinsky to pose for him. The sittings were interrupted and a finished statue never emerged, but this small study owes its effectiveness partly to its roughness of execution. Handling his material with a force still evident in the traces of finger marks, Rodin caught Nijinsky's unmistakable physical traits: the Oriental cast of his face, his muscular neck, his powerful torso and overdeveloped legs. Viewed from any angle, as these photographs reveal, the figure expresses the faun's rapacious, primitive potency.

VII

Gift to the Future

At the peak of his fame in his late sixties, Rodin nearly toppled from
the pinnacle he had so long sought. He had, in effect, two simultaneous
affairs of the heart: one with the decaying Hôtel Biron, a two-century-
old mansion in the center of Paris, the other with the grasping Duchesse
de Choiseul, a fortyish woman whose charms, like the Biron's, lay large-
ly in the past. Between them, mansion and mistress almost undid the
greatest sculptor of the age.

Of the two, the Biron was by far the more attractive. Set in its own 17-
acre park, the house had many huge rooms, now almost bare, and a décor and stately façade dating back to Louis XV. Formerly owned by a
succession of wealthy families, it had gradually deteriorated, serving in
the 19th Century as a convent school. As Church property, it had recently been expropriated, along with many other holdings, by an anti-
clerical French government and had become a flaking, leaking ward of
the state. The state had no clear notion of what to do with it other than
try to gain some revenue from it; there was talk of razing it and breaking up the park into building lots. Meanwhile rooms and apartments
could be rented in the mansion, if one were willing to overlook its lack
of adequate heating and plumbing.

A number of writers and artists did so, drawn both to the low rents
(the state took whatever it could get) and to the sequestered environment; with its untended gardens and high wall, the place had an air
of bucolic isolation. The precocious Jean Cocteau, still a student when
he moved in but soon to emerge as a poet and playwright, wrote that it
was "a spectacle of silence [giving] the visual feeling of being a thou-
sand miles from Paris, right out in the country." The painter Henri Matisse was another tenant. The actor Édouard de Max, known for his
boisterous homosexual parties, settled in and converted a former chapel into an ornate Roman-style bath; Isadora Duncan held dancing classes
on the splintering parquet floor of a long, glassed-in gallery. The poet Rainer Maria Rilke, whom Rodin had abruptly fired as his secretary in 1906,
took quarters on the ground floor.

In 1908, still grieving at his separation from Rodin and knowing the sculptor's love of old houses, Rilke suggested that he, too, take up residence at the Biron. Rodin needed only one look, and promptly took over a large part of the main floor at an annual rental of 5,900 francs (which made him the highest-paying tenant). Rilke gave him a housewarming present—a 16th Century statuette of St. Christopher bearing the Christ Child—and effusively likened the piece to "Rodin carrying his work. It becomes increasingly heavy, but it contains the world."

In time Rodin's new setting was to arouse in him the thought that here he might assemble his life's work and his collections and deed them to the French state and people, provided the Biron were converted into a museum to house them. But at first he saw the place as just another haven for both work and women—more of the latter, it turned out, than the former. The Biron became Rodin's last playground. He still had possession of the Dépôt des Marbres studio in the nearby Rue de l'Université that the government had granted for his use at the outset of his commission for *The Gates of Hell*. Cluttered with the accumulation of years, this studio had up to now served as his Paris base; he had customarily visited it several times a week for a change of scene from his country seat at Meudon, where he maintained Rose. But in both places he had apparently begun to feel more and more confined, despite his claim that he was now in search of "serenity." With his move to the Biron, it soon became clear that he was not really interested in serenity. For fully four years he abandoned Meudon, communicating with Rose only through an assistant.

The chief cause of this estrangement was the American-born Duchesse de Choiseul, whom Rodin had met several years before in company with her parasitic husband, an improvident gambler. The former Claire Coudert, daughter of a socially prominent New York attorney, the Duchess was neither a *grande dame* nor the kind of stylish beauty Rodin had often idolized. Squat, heavily painted, noisy, bursting with animal spirits, she was a distinctly raffish type, something of an international tramp. Judith Cladel, who always tried to preserve her composure while watching the parade of Rodin's mistresses, lost some of it when observing this latest addition—"a music hall girl who has become a demi-mondaine," ruffling the master's white hair with her diamond-studded fingers, insulting the servants at the Biron "with the hauteur of a parvenue." Rodin's other friends were equally appalled at his infatuation with the Duchess and the way she began to run his life.

She was half drunk part of the time. "I am your Muse," she exclaimed to Rodin, "I am the reincarnation of your lost sister." She would turn on the gramophone and dance for him, flinging her scarf about gracelessly and afterward collapsing, breathless, on a couch. She argued that he must place his business affairs in her hands, that she could bring him rich patrons from America. She warned him against his friends: they were all, she said, disloyal to him. She so effectively isolated Rodin that on one occasion she turned away two of his closest friends—one the rising sculptor Aristide Maillol—even as Rodin sat in the garden of the Biron awaiting them.

Nevertheless, he reveled in her ministrations. He described her as his "little bacchante" and "my amazing little friend who dances with passionate ardor," coming forward "like Minerva of bygone days" with a "conquering smile . . . a proud caryatid." They traveled together to the South of France (he was interested in seeing more old churches); they visited Rome and met wealthy Americans there. But there were flaws in the idyl. The few old friends who still were allowed to see Rodin soon noticed that after a round of pleasure he would sink into torpor and depression, even into drink. Stories spread that the Duchess was quietly stealing from him, and the reports were accurate; rolls of drawings vanished under her wraps whenever she left the Biron. She was reported as boasting that "I handle everything for Rodin; I *am* Rodin!" Rodin ignored or dismissed secretaries at her bidding.

Still, despite Rodin's apparent lapse into senility, he showed recurrent flashes of the old creativity. His sculptures were few, compared to the output of earlier years, but several were notable. Even while bewitched by his Duchess, he had the clarity to make two heads of her that were masterly in their psychological dissection: she appears not as a charming nymph but as a jaded worldling. His long-standing interest in the arts of the East quickened when he met Hanako, a diminutive Japanese dancer and actress *(page 140)*. In a series of swift studies that probed beneath the formality of Hanako's Oriental reserve, Rodin caught a wide range of emotions. And in the following year, despite the distractions of his Duchess, he modeled one of his most commanding heads—that of the Austrian composer Gustav Mahler.

The sittings took place in Rodin's rooms at the Biron. Rodin and Mahler, both great romantics, both turbulent rebels drawn to the grandiose and the exotic, had much in common, but nothing is recorded of what they talked about. The sittings were attended by Mahler's extraordinary wife, Alma, who after his death became, successively, the wife of the architect Walter Gropius and of the novelist Franz Werfel. In her memoirs Alma recalled only that Rodin was busy "rubbing tiny balls of clay between his fingers," and that while he was so absorbed "there was always one of his mistresses waiting next door" (presumably the Duchess). Rodin did tell her, Alma remembered, that Mahler's head, with its deep brow, struck him as a composite of those of Mozart, Frederick the Great and Benjamin Franklin; the lean, intense portrait Rodin produced, however, is a striking study in individuality *(page 83)*.

Another celebrity who came to pose for a bust by Rodin was Georges Clemenceau, who by now enjoyed the status of ex-Premier of France. Clemenceau had 18 sittings in 1911, but when the head was completed he detested it. It made him, he snorted, look like a Mongolian general —and indeed it did *(page 83)*. When Rodin showed it at the Salon, Clemenceau insisted that it be titled simply *Bust of an Unknown.* This ruse deceived nobody, for Rodin had discerned and caught the curiously Oriental cast and savage power of the man who, when he again served as Premier of France during World War I, came to be known as the Tiger.

There were further indications that Rodin had not entirely lost his old spirit. As the war neared, emissaries of Kaiser Wilhelm II called on him. The German emperor held strong views on art, reactionary ones, and had frowned on Rodin's work when it was first exhibited across the Rhine. But the sculptor's fame was now such that His Imperial Majesty was actually ready to come to Paris to sit for a bust. A price was agreed on but Rodin had an afterthought: would it really be proper for him to portray a man who was certainly no friend of France? At the last minute he pleaded ill health and turned down the honor. One can only speculate about what he might have done with the arrogant Hohenzollern features.

Other sitters, other projects, proved more palatable. Rodin experienced one particularly joyous burst of activity in 1912 while the phenomenal Vaslav Nijinsky was performing in Paris as star of Sergei Diaghilev's Ballets Russes. For Rodin, a lover of the dance, the troupe's appearance in the French capital inspired his most brilliant dance sculpture. It also caused him some unexpected personal anguish.

The sensational highlight of the visit of the Ballets Russes was the première of the ballet *The Afternoon of a Faun*, set to the music of Claude Debussy. As the faun, Nijinsky delighted some spectators by his dazzling leaps and daring displays, and outraged others by what a critic in *Le Figaro* called his "vile movements of erotic bestiality and gestures of unmitigated lewdness." All Paris, it seemed, took up arms for or against Nijinsky. Another cultural *scandale* was at hand, and Rodin found himself in the thick of it when he put his name to an article in *Le Matin* hailing the dancer as an apostle of "freedom of instinct" like Isadora Duncan and Loie Fuller, a battler in the struggle against the forces of prejudice and inertia.

In gratitude for this defense Nijinsky came to dance for Rodin on a number of occasions. Rodin made many quick drawings of these performances, and then produced a figure that was the very essence of the man—a contorted, whirling, bounding shape, all but free of gravity, the whole compass of his demonic movements seen as if at once, all violence and grace *(pages 162-163)*. One of the sessions, however, ended very badly indeed. The day was hot; the two men drank a good deal of wine at lunch after their exertions and then lay down to rest. Suddenly someone walked in unannounced; it was Diaghilev, who was deeply jealous of Rodin's relationship with his star. When he found the two men asleep, Nijinsky at Rodin's feet, he leaped to conclusions and stormed out. Soon Paris heard of a breach between dancer and impresario, and buzzed with the report that the third party was Rodin, caught *in flagrante*. "*I* a pederast!" Rodin could only exclaim in shock.

The incident could not have occurred at a worse time for him. The tenants of the Biron had been given eviction notices; the state was considering using it as a public building. This was the turn of events that stirred Rodin's interest in restoring the place at his own expense and making it into a museum to house the works he intended to bequeath to the state. The ever faithful Judith Cladel toured numerous ministries on his behalf; in the intricate forest of French bureaucracy, there were several that would have to assent to his proposal—Fine Arts, Public Instruction, Finance, Commerce, even Religious Affairs (because the Biron was expropriated Church property). Approval by Paris municipal authorities was also necessary before the final step, an en-

Ernest Durig, photographed with Rodin in 1915, was a Swiss sculptor who supported himself for 30 years by faking Rodin's drawings, sculpture and handwriting. In addition to signing his fraudulent works with Rodin's name, Durig was adept at doctoring authentic letters so that they appeared to be addressed to him or to praise him. Very likely he forged this photograph's inscription, "Your Admirer, Rodin."

abling act by the French parliament. Judith enlisted the support of such key political leaders as Clemenceau and Aristide Briand, but a virulent conservative opposition to Rodin, quiescent since the furor over his Balzac monument, now made itself heard. His foes assailed the idea of preserving the Biron as a showplace for him—not only because of his reported wealth, but also because of his intimacy with the supposed libertine Nijinsky and because of his defacement of the former convent school with "libidinous" work. The rightists and the righteous shrewdly scented fair game in the bohemian goings on at the Biron. The influential *Le Figaro* published a caricature that showed a model undressing and asking Rodin where to put her clothes. "Over there," the leering sculptor replies, "in the chapel."

Eager to realize his dream for a museum, Rodin made an abject gesture of surrender. Encouraged by his Duchess, he disavowed his *Matin* article in praise of Nijinsky (it had been written for his signature by his longtime friend, the critic Roger Marx) and suggested that he had never been all that enthusiastic about the dancer's work. This action cost Rodin more friends and cast doubt upon his mental stability. Public officials who were considering his Biron proposal suddenly suspended their deliberations.

The drawing above is a genuine Rodin. Below is a forgery by Ernest Durig. Most of Durig's fakes are of dancers or nudes—favorite Rodin subjects—but Durig lacked Rodin's grasp of the dynamics of the body and his genius for harmonizing its proportions to produce a free-flowing form. Compared with Rodin's nude, Durig's is stiff, fussy and unnaturally balanced; even the drapery is contrived. Although some Durig forgeries are more convincing, most are crude and ungainly.

Rodin, however, was not losing his senses but regaining them. Apparently the Nijinsky affair, the rumors that he was becoming a drunkard and the loss of some of his friends combined to shake him hard. He abruptly banished the Duchess from the Biron. Reportedly he did not quite have the courage to do so himself; a friend was asked to bundle her out with orders never to return. She never did, and Rodin moved back to Meudon. He had been gone from it for four years but Rose, again the patient victor over one of Rodin's women, was waiting for him at the end of the avenue of chestnut trees. They greeted each other—"Bon soir, Rose"—"Bon soir, mon ami"—and went indoors, arm in arm.

He never again left Rose and Meudon for any length of time. On one of his brief trips away from home, to Picardy, he wrote her a particularly touching love letter of old age: "I send you this letter as a reflection of the greatness of the gift God made in placing you close to me. Place this in your generous heart. I shall return Tuesday. Your beloved, Auguste Rodin."

Soon after their reconciliation Rodin suffered a slight stroke that left an arm temporarily paralyzed. He was so terrified that he gave up drinking and went on a diet in which milk was the chief ingredient—a sure-fire cure for incipient alcoholism, the French then believed. With his vigor restored, he enthusiastically launched on a project long dear to his heart—the collection of his observations of the cathedrals of France. In visiting them over the years, with Rose or Camille or the Duchess, Rodin had made numbers of swift architectural sketches, and set down some notes as well—mere jottings, often ungrammatical ("I have no need of grammar, that children's nurse"). He now worked with a writer friend, Charles Morice, to put all this into book form.

Appearing in 1914, *The Cathedrals of France* was a moving paean to French medieval art as the unique and superlative embodiment of the na-

169

tion's genius. Scores of drawings illustrated a thought-provoking text. "The Cathedral is a synthesis of our country," Rodin declared. "All of our France is in our cathedrals, just as all of Greece is summarized in the Parthenon." He dwelt rhapsodically on the debt of medieval carvers to the flowering fields of France. He wrote of the beauty of sculptural shadows falling at twilight, of church bells ringing, of crisply dressed girls going to First Communion. He denounced the prevalent neglect of France's great churches and the tasteless efforts at their restoration. "To bring our people to the Cathedral," Rodin summed up, "is to lead them home, to their dwelling, to the citadel of their power. The country cannot perish so long as the Cathedrals endure. They are our Muses. They are our Mothers." Rodin's book was widely hailed. The year of its publication was one in which appeals to patriotism had a special validity. Within months, a number of the great shrines of France were being battered and besieged by advancing German armies, and the sculptor's invocation was remembered.

The ardor of his expression suggested to some people that he might be embarking on a new phase of creativity. But the book was in effect his swan song—the final strong statement of a man who was beginning to decline. He grew increasingly erratic, unable to handle his business affairs. In view of the value now attached to anything bearing Rodin's mark or signature, his collection of his own works became a hunting ground for all manner of alleged friends and rank impostors. (One caller, a Swiss named Ernest Durig, contrived to get himself photographed with Rodin and, billing himself as the sculptor's "last pupil," earned a living for 30 years peddling forgeries of Rodin drawings.)

Rodin himself, assisted by Judith Cladel and other supporters, still pursued his museum scheme. An agreement with the government ministries concerned was almost reached in the summer of 1914, but when war broke out in early August the French state had more urgent matters to attend to. Ludicrously, Rodin went on importuning the government during the first desperate days of the German advance. By September, the enemy threatened to envelop Paris and its environs, and the Biron itself was designated a command post. Rodin fearfully fled to England, the scene of so many of his past triumphs. With Rose and Judith Cladel and her mother, he took refuge in a country hotel in Gloucestershire. He was gloomy and withdrawn, emerging from his shell only to take tea downstairs with the elderly lady guests.

After the German march on Paris was halted, he moved on, traveling by rail across France to Rome, where a commission to sculpt Pope Benedict XV awaited him. The visit was a failure. Rodin arrived in November 1914. Although Italy did not enter the war on the Allied side until the following year, the Romans were too preoccupied with following the hostilities to pay court to him. Moreover, the Pope was too busy to sit, and Rodin was obliged to postpone the project for several months. When at last it got underway, Benedict in turn became annoyed with Rodin, who insisted on viewing his skull from above (the Pontiff thought it unseemly for anyone to look down on the head of the Church). "Finish, finish, Monsieur Rodin," the Pope said impatiently after four

The newly married Rodins posed for this
photograph in their drawing room at Meudon
a few hours after the ceremony, which was
held at the villa because of Rose's sinking
health. The date was January 29, 1917, some
52 years after she had become Rodin's
mistress, model and housekeeper. During the
ceremony, asked if she would take Rodin as
her husband, Rose placed a hand on her breast
and quavered: "Yes . . . with all my heart."

sittings, and no further sessions were held. Rodin went back to France
with his clay model; later cast in bronze, the unfinished head is a work
of considerable force.

After Rodin returned to Meudon in April 1915, he began to slide down-
hill, mentally and physically. The war had settled into bloody stalemate
in the trenches along the Western Front, but the French parliament
had still not passed the enabling act to establish the Rodin Museum.
Rodin himself was partly to blame; he raised countless, querulous objections to ideas set forth by the various ministries concerned. In the
spring of 1916 he signed a provisional contract—drawn up by the ministries—leaving his estate to France. What it consisted of no one knew

Rodin was always entranced by the beauty of French cathedrals, and visited them periodically as a welcome change from his grueling labors in Paris. Below and on the opposite page are some of the drawings of cathedral architecture that he made on his trips and later published in a book, *The Cathedrals of France*. The first sketch below shows the Gothic portal of a church in Houdan, the next a 17th Century portal of a church in Toulouse. Opposite, from the top, are decorative details from churches Rodin saw in Quimperlé, Caen and Étampes.

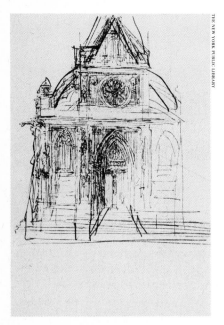

THE NEW YORK PUBLIC LIBRARY

—least of all Rodin himself, who could not recall even the names of the banks in which he had deposited his supposedly vast earnings (shortly before his death it was determined that his holdings in cash and securities consisted of 350,000 francs, the equivalent of $60,000 at the time). Meanwhile, many of Rodin's possessions disappeared from both Meudon and the Paris studio. Ex-mistresses or agents of ex-mistresses appeared to collect their share of loot. Corrupt servants let in interlopers, possibly including some dispatched by the discarded Duchess of Choiseul and her Duke. The dancer Loie Fuller arrived at Meudon to make a claim in person, only to leave angrily when told that Rodin's treasures were to be given to the state.

In July 1916 Rodin suffered another stroke. Upon his recovery, he would wander about abstractedly, and officials of the ministries were fearful that in an erratic moment he might change his mind about his bequest. They persuaded him to sign a will naming Rose Beuret as heir, with the understanding that she, in turn, would leave everything to the state. This document he signed with a wavering hand. The incumbent Minister of Commerce, Étienne Clémentel, arranged that henceforth Rodin be placed under the care of a nurse with specific instructions that he not be given access to a pen: otherwise he might attempt to make still another will, to the detriment of the state. Finally, in the depths of the war—December 1916—came passage of the enabling act accepting Rodin's gift to the nation. He watched, a bewildered old man, as some of his favorite Meudon possessions were trucked off to Paris.

Apparently it was Judith Cladel who first advanced the suggestion that if Rodin had made Rose his heir, he might also at last dignify their relationship by marrying her. Rodin smilingly agreed. So these curiously matched companions of half a century—Rose now 72, Rodin 76—were married by the mayor of Meudon early in 1917. Rose, arousing herself from a sickbed, wore her best frilled dress. Rodin appeared in his flopping velvet cap and sat gazing at a Van Gogh in the drawing room at Meudon until time came to take the vows. Afterward, champagne was served to a small company of friends. Two weeks later, Rose was dead of pneumonia. "How beautiful she is—a piece of sculpture," Rodin remarked as he viewed her on her deathbed.

He did not long outlive her. That spring and summer the house was further emptied as his remaining life's work was carried away under the terms of his gift. By autumn, Rodin was left with little but the vigilant company of a nurse. There was not a pad or a pencil in reach. Of more importance, there was little coal; the Ministry of Commerce had neglected to supply it. Rodin's doctor warned that he should be moved to a warmer climate; the late fall was cold and grim, and there was almost no heat in the old house. Swaddled in wraps, enfeebled, desolate, Rodin one night in November murmured some compliment about the work of Puvis de Chavannes, a fellow artist, and died.

Some weeks earlier, emissaries from the Institut de France, the official arbiter of the arts in France, had notified him that he was at last up for election to membership in that august body. Whether Rodin was lucid on the occasion is not known, although he nodded his assent.

His election was to have been voted on November 23. But his death came six days earlier, and so this ultimate accolade was denied him. The French Republic, desperately engaged in fighting for its own survival, did not give him a state funeral, but it did bury him with the tricolor of France. On his bier lay the red sash of a Grand Officer of the Legion of Honor and the red robe of his doctorate from Oxford. His favorite cast of *The Thinker* brooded over the grave site at Meudon.

Seldom was an artist so prized in his lifetime; seldom, also, did one so soon fall into disfavor. Rodin's reputation began to slip almost immediately after his death. For a while, at least, he was destined to be bypassed if not altogether rejected. A few followers like Bourdelle and Despiau remained faithful to his precepts. But more notable sculptors veered from the path he had set. Artistic meaning was now to be sought and found outside the realm of representation and literary allusion.

In time the influential English critic Kenneth Clark consigned Rodin to limbo as one "with whom an epoch and an episode have come to an end." In a sense, this is true: Rodin was the last major sculptor to concern himself with literary or classical motifs. But he was also a Janus figure, looking both to the past and to the future. He taught sculptors that they need not limit themselves in expressing their views of man's estate. He gave the world of sculpture a new sense of freedom, and all its subsequent practitioners are, knowingly or unknowingly, in his debt. One of the most talented of them, Jacques Lipchitz, acknowledged this fact in 1962, almost half a century after his death. Even after so many years, Lipchitz confessed, he could not rid himself of a kind of guilt complex toward Rodin, and explained why.

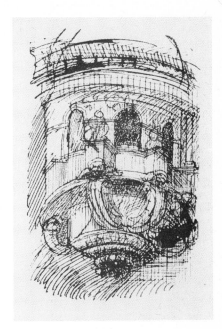

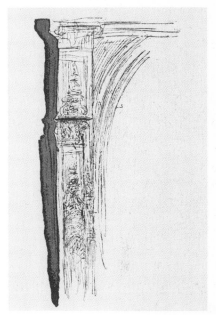

When he arrived in Paris as a very young sculptor, he recalled, he could "neither understand nor grasp the immense chaotic richness which Rodin's *oeuvre* embodies. . . . I fled from him. I remember a story which even today makes me blush with shame. In 1912, at the Salon National des Beaux-Arts of which Rodin was president, I exhibited two heads. . . . My friend the sculptor Léon Cladel [brother of Judith Cladel] . . . was asked that year to receive the President during his visit to the opening. Naturally I ran away. . . . Returning after the presidential visit, I saw my friend Cladel running toward me, all flushed with [excitement]. 'Rodin,' he told me, 'has noticed your little bronze head, and he asked me to tell you that if you work hard, something will become of you.' Incredible as it must seem, this news made me deadly sad. I asked myself, 'What could be so wrong with my little sculpture that Rodin liked it?'

"It was only during the First World War . . . that I could visit the Musée Rodin. My joy was immense, and so was my enthusiasm at finding so many riches. . . . These figures without arms, heads and legs were endowed with a sense of mystery, and one needed imagination to complete the figure, . . . at that moment I understood that a work of art needs . . . mystery. I clearly saw that what Rodin was doing instinctively was not so different from what we, the Cubists, were doing in a more intellectual way. . . . he was more advanced than we . . . he surpassed anything done in his time, either in painting or sculpture."

A Liberating Legacy

Rodin actively worked at his art as late as the second decade of the 20th Century, but more and more he fell out of step with the new forces sweeping sculpture. Just as he himself had challenged mid-19th Century tradition, so younger sculptors spurned his style in a widening search for their own means of expression. They not only generally reacted against him as the dominant figure of their times, but specifically rejected his realism, his emotionalism, and the literary or thematic character of most of his work. Insulated from this new world by success and a host of hero-worshipers, Rodin became an old master, a museum piece.

Responding to the quickened pace of life and the growing impact of science and technology, 20th Century sculpture evolved rapidly. Its practitioners, believing that the problems of realistic rendering had been solved, moved principally toward abstraction. Picasso and Lipchitz shattered form into Cubist planes. Maillol and Moore reduced the human figure to its essentials. Boccioni captured the elusive element of speed. Giacometti evoked the terror of dreams in three dimensions. Brancusi and Arp modeled free forms based on organic shapes. Gabo employed materials never before used in sculpture, and Calder made it move. In the first half of the 20th Century the art saw more innovations than in most of its thousands of years of history. Adored or derided, the man who paved the way for this phenomenon was Rodin.

A Rodin assistant who became a teacher and respected sculptor in his own right, Antoine Bourdelle retained some of the elements of the master's style. This warrior shows both the detailed musculature and intensity of emotion that mark Rodin's most dramatic works.

Émile-Antoine Bourdelle: *The Warrior*, bronze, 1900
JOSEPH H. HIRSHHORN COLLECTION

174

Pablo Picasso: *Head of a Woman*, bronze, 1906

A concern with the play of light on varied surfaces—one of Rodin's main preoccupations—absorbed many subsequent artists as well. Henri Matisse, who studied with Bourdelle for a time and was thus directly linked to Rodin's teachings, showed this influence in the rough texture of his *Slave (left)*. Although in his paintings Matisse increasingly favored flat planes, he periodically turned to sculpture to refresh his acquaintance with three-dimensional form.

Another sculpture clearly in Rodin's tradition is Sir Jacob Epstein's study of the novelist Joseph Conrad at right. As in Rodin's perceptive portrait busts, Epstein's vigorous modeling of his sitter's features to produce shadow and highlight serves to add to the viewer's appreciation of the character behind the face.

The broken surfaces of the woman's head above, by Picasso, had a purpose far different from any envisioned by Rodin. As innovative a sculptor as he was a painter, Picasso fashioned this bust not as a study in light and shade or as a character portrayal but as a demonstration of the theory of Cubism. By fracturing the basic structure of the head into facets, Picasso produced a strictly geometric analysis of form.

Henri Matisse: *The Slave*, bronze, 1900-1903

Jacob Epstein: *Joseph Conrad*, bronze, 1924-1925

Henry Moore: *Reclining Figure*, lead, 1938

Aristide Maillol: *The River*, lead, 1939-1943

Partly in reaction against Rodin's emphasis on realistic detail and surface texture, sculptors began to simplify form dramatically in dealing with the human figure. The Frenchman Aristide Maillol, who turned from painting to sculpture around 1900, summed up his differences with his friend Rodin in this way: "I was trying to simplify, whereas he noted all the profiles, all the details. It was a matter of conscience." Maillol's favorite subject was the female figure. He created scores of statuesque women, seeing them not as portraits of individuals, but as ample, sturdy figures who represented elemental concepts, as in *The River (right, below)*. In spite of their evocative titles, Maillol's robust nudes are primarily frank celebrations of the lush curves of the mature female.

Henry Moore, the contemporary English sculptor, has moved still further from Rodin's realism by abstracting the basic forms of the human body, piercing and stretching them almost unrecognizably. The distortions of Moore's figures also give them an emotional quality—often of isolation or despair—that is typical of the response of many artists to the complexity and brutality of 20th Century life.

178

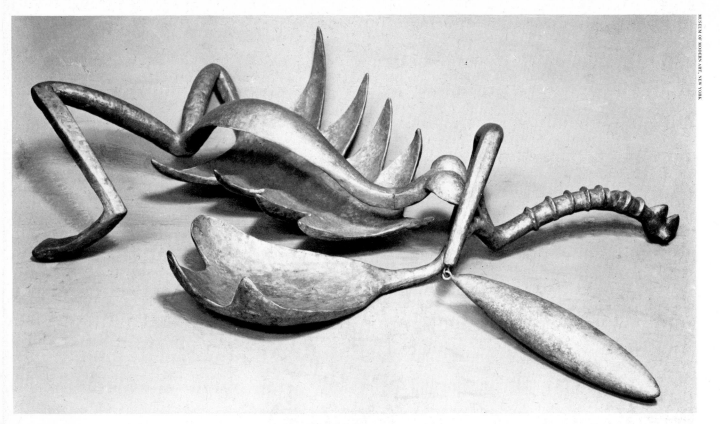

Alberto Giacometti: *Woman with Her Throat Cut*, bronze, 1932

Jacques Lipchitz: *Reclining Nude with Guitar*, bronze, 1928

As the 20th Century progressed, sculptors intensified their search for new ways to represent the figure. Umberto Boccioni, a member of a group called The Futurists, expressed the speed of the machine age in the fluid action of the form at left. It offers a parallel to Rodin's *Walking Man (page 81)*, and is no less successful as a study of motion. Jacques Lipchitz examined the body in Cubist terms and produced a whimsical amalgam of geometric forms which integrates female curves with those of a guitar *(above)*. Alberto Giacometti delved into the Freud-inspired dream world of Surrealism when he created the macabre image of the woman at top. While still concerned with the human figure, sculpture became a wider medium for personal expression.

Umberto Boccioni: *Unique Forms of Continuity in Space*, bronze, 1913

Jean Arp: *Growth*, bronze, 1938

Although Rodin viewed some of his sculptured fragments—his legless torsos and disembodied limbs—as finished works, it remained for others to go the whole distance toward abstraction. In Paris, after the turn of the century, the young Rumanian Constantin Brancusi fell under Rodin's influence briefly, but in time he turned to a fiercely individual style of radical simplification. The photograph at left of a Brancusi exhibit in 1955 shows his small blocklike *The Kiss (foreground)*, resembling some primitive monument; behind it is an elegantly polished marble called *The Miracle* or *Seal*, and in the background the totemic wooden *Caryatid*.

German-born Jean Arp, once described as a "one-man laboratory for the discovery of new form," produced the gleaming, richly rounded bronze above. It is one of hundreds of Arp's experiments with organic shapes.

A Brancusi Exhibition at the Guggenheim Museum, New York

Naum Gabo: *Linear Construction, Number 1*, plastic, 1942-1943

Once tradition's hold on sculpture had been broken, new ideas and techniques followed in dizzying profusion. Abandoning bronze or marble and age-old methods of modeling or carving, a group called the Constructivists made geometric abstractions from such materials as plastic and sheet metal. "Sculpture of mass is dependent on lighting," wrote two of the group's leaders, Naum Gabo and Antoine Pevsner, "while our constructions carry shadow and light within themselves"—a claim borne out in Gabo's elegant plastic structure above.

Another challenge to convention came from the American Alexander Calder, who decided that sculpture concerned with motion and space should *move* in space. Calder's often humorously titled free-form metal "mobiles" *(right)* are delicately balanced on wires, and swing in the lightest breeze. What Rodin would have thought of such efforts is unknown. But his own trail blazing made the 20th Century revolution possible.

Alexander Calder: *Lobster Trap and Fish Tail*, steel wire and sheet aluminum, 1939

Chronology: Artists of Rodin's Era

FRANCE

CLODION (CLAUDE MICHEL)	1738-1814
JEAN-ANTOINE HOUDON	1741-1828
JEAN-AUGUSTE DOMINIQUE INGRES	1780-1867
FRANÇOIS RUDE	1784-1855
DAVID D'ANGERS (PIERRE-JEAN DAVID)	1789-1856
THÉODORE GÉRICAULT	1791-1824
JEAN-JACQUES (JAMES) PRADIER	1792-1852
ANTOINE-LOUIS BARYE	1796-1875
HONORÉ DAUMIER	1808-1879
AUGUSTE PRÉAULT	1809-1879
FÉLIX-JOSEPH BARRIAS	1822-1907
ALBERT-ERNEST CARRIÈRE-BELLEUSE	1824-1887
PIERRE PUVIS DE CHAVANNES	1824-1898
JEAN-BAPTISTE CARPEAUX	1827-1875
JEAN-ALEXANDRE-JOSEPH FALGUIÈRE	1831-1900
ÉDOUARD MANET	1832-1883
HENRI CHAPU	1833-1891
FRÉDÉRIC-AUGUSTE BARTHOLDI	1834-1904
EDGAR DEGAS	1834-1917
ALPHONSE LEGROS	1837-1911
JULES DALOU	1838-1902
PAUL CÉZANNE	1839-1906
AUGUSTE RODIN	1840-1917
MARQUET DE VASSELOT	1840-1904
PIERRE-AUGUSTE RENOIR	1841-1919
MARIUS J. ANTONIN MERCIÉ	1845-1916
ALBERT BARTHOLOMÉ	1848-1928
PAUL GAUGUIN	1848-1903
EUGÈNE CARRIÈRE	1849-1906
JULES DESBOIS	1851-1935
ARISTIDE MAILLOL	1861-1944
ÉMILE-ANTOINE BOURDELLE	1861-1929
HENRI MATISSE	1869-1954
CHARLES DESPIAU	1874-1946
CONSTANTIN BRANCUSI	1876-1957
RAYMOND DUCHAMP-VILLON	1876-1918
ANDRÉ DERAIN	1880-1954
GEORGES BRAQUE	1882-1963
HENRI LAURENS	1885-1954
MARCEL DUCHAMP	1887-1968
JEAN ARP	1888-1966
JACQUES LIPCHITZ	1891-

ITALY

ANTONIO CANOVA	1757-1822
CARLO CARRÀ	1881-1966
UMBERTO BOCCIONI	1882-1916
GINO SEVERINI	1883-1966
AMEDEO MODIGLIANI	1884-1920

HOLLAND

VINCENT VAN GOGH	1853-1890
PIET MONDRIAN	1872-1944
GEORGES VANTONGERLOO	1886-

BELGIUM

CONSTANTIN MEUNIER	1831-1905
JAMES ENSOR	1860-1949
GEORGE MINNE	1866-1941

GERMANY

GOTTFRIED SCHADOW	1764-1850
ADOLF VON HILDEBRAND	1847-1921
ERNST BARLACH	1870-1938
GEORG KOLBE	1877-1947
WILHELM LEHMBRUCK	1881-1919
MAX BECKMANN	1884-1950
KURT SCHWITTERS	1887-1948
MAX ERNST	1891-

SWITZERLAND

PAUL KLEE	1879-1940
ALBERTO GIACOMETTI	1901-1966

ENGLAND

WILLIAM HOLMAN HUNT	1827-1910
DANTE GABRIEL ROSSETTI	1828-1882
JOHN EVERETT MILLAIS	1829-1896
EDWARD BURNE-JONES	1833-1898
WALTER SICKERT	1860-1942
JACOB EPSTEIN	1880-1959
BEN NICHOLSON	1894-
HENRY MOORE	1898-
BARBARA HEPWORTH	1903-

SCANDINAVIA

JOHAN TOBIAS SERGEL (SWEDEN)	1740-1814
BERTEL THORVALDSEN (DENMARK)	1768-1844
EDVARD MUNCH (NORWAY)	1863-1944
GUSTAV VIGELAND (NORWAY)	1869-1943
CARL MILLES (SWEDEN)	1875-1955

SPAIN

JULIO GONZÁLEZ	1876-1942
PABLO PICASSO	1881-
JOAN MIRÓ	1893-

EASTERN EUROPE AND RUSSIA

WASSILY KANDINSKY	1866-1944
VLADIMIR TATLIN	1885-1953
ANTOINE PEVSNER	1886-1962
ALEXANDER ARCHIPENKO	1887-1964
MARC CHAGALL	1889-
NAUM GABO	1890-

UNITED STATES

WILLIAM RIMMER	1816-1879
JAMES ABBOTT MCNEILL WHISTLER	1834-1905
WINSLOW HOMER	1836-1910
THOMAS EAKINS	1844-1916
AUGUSTUS SAINT-GAUDENS	1848-1907
DANIEL CHESTER FRENCH	1850-1932
JOHN SINGER SARGENT	1856-1925
LORADO TAFT	1860-1936
FREDERIC REMINGTON	1861-1909
ARTHUR B. DAVIES	1862-1928
CHARLES RUSSELL	1865-1926
GUTZON BORGLUM	1867-1941
A. STIRLING CALDER	1870-1945
ANNA VAUGHN HYATT (HUNTINGTON)	1876-
GASTON LACHAISE	1882-1935
MALVINA HOFFMAN	1887-1966
ALEXANDER CALDER	1898-

Rodin's predecessors, contemporaries and successors are grouped chronologically by country. The bands correspond to the artists' life spans.

Bibliography

*Available in paperback

RODIN—HIS LIFE AND WORK

Baudelaire, Charles, *Les Fleurs du Mal*. Illustrated by Auguste Rodin. Limited Editions Club, Paris, 1940.

Champigneulle, Bernard, *Rodin: His Sculptures, Drawings and Watercolors*. Translated by J. Maxwell Brownjohn. Harry N. Abrams, Inc., 1967.

Cladel, Judith:
   Rodin. Translated by James Whitall. Harcourt, Brace & Co., 1937.
   Rodin: The Man and His Art. Translated by S. K. Star. The Century Co., 1917.

Descharnes, Robert, and Jean-François Chabrun, *Auguste Rodin*. The Viking Press, 1967.

Elsen, Albert E.:
   Rodin. The Museum of Modern Art, 1963.
   Rodin's Gates of Hell. University of Minnesota Press, 1960.

Elsen, Albert E. (editor), *Auguste Rodin: Readings on His Life and Works.* * Essays by T. H. Bartlett, Rainer Maria Rilke and Henri Dujardin-Beaumetz. Prentice-Hall, Inc., 1965.

Geissbuhler, Elisabeth Chase, *Rodin, Later Drawings*. With interpretations by Antoine Bourdelle. Beacon Press, 1963.

Goldscheider, Cécile, *Rodin: sa vie, son oeuvre, son héritage*. Les Productions de Paris, Paris, 1962.

Gsell, Paul (editor), *Art by Auguste Rodin*. Translated by Mrs. Romilly Fedden. Small, Maynard & Co., 1916.

Lawton, Frederick, *The Life and Work of Auguste Rodin*. Charles Scribner's, 1907.

Ludovici, Anthony, *Personal Reminiscences of Auguste Rodin*. John Murray, London, 1926.

Rilke, Rainer Maria, *Auguste Rodin*. Translated by Jessie Lemont and Hans Trausil. Greywall Press, London, 1946.

Rodin, Auguste, *Cathedrals of France*. Translated by Elisabeth Chase Geissbuhler. Beacon Press, 1965.

Rodin Sculptures and Drawings. Introduction by Leo Steinberg. Charles E. Slatkin Galleries, 1963.

Sutton, Denys, *Triumphant Satyr: The World of Auguste Rodin*. Country Life Limited, London, 1966.

ART—HISTORICAL BACKGROUND

Bazin, Germain, *The History of World Sculpture*. New York Graphic Society, 1968.
Eaton, D. Cady, *A Handbook of Modern French Sculpture*. Dodd, Mead, 1913.
Hamilton, George Heard, *Painting and Sculpture in Europe: 1880-1940*. The Pelican History of Art Series. Penguin Books, Inc., 1967.

Hoffman, Malvina, *Sculpture Inside and Out*. W. W. Norton & Co., Inc., 1939.

Le Dix-neuvième Siècle Français. Collection Connaissance des Arts. Librairie Hachette, Paris, 1957.

Licht, Fred, *Sculpture, 19th and 20th Centuries*. Consultant-editor John Pope-Hennessy. New York Graphic Society, 1967.

Modern Sculpture from the Joseph H. Hirshhorn Collection. The Solomon R. Guggenheim Foundation, 1962.

Molesworth, H. D., *European Sculpture from Romanesque to Neoclassic.* * Frederick A. Praeger, Publishers, 1965.

Novotny, Fritz, *Painting and Sculpture in Europe: 1780-1880*. The Pelican History of Art Series. Penguin Books, Inc., 1960.

Ritchie, Andrew Carnduff, *Sculpture of the Twentieth Century*. The Museum of Modern Art, 1952.

Savage, George, *A Concise History of Bronzes.* * Frederick A. Praeger, Publishers, 1969.

Selz, Jean, *Modern Sculpture*. Translated by Annette Michelson. George Braziller, Inc., 1963.

Seymour, Charles, *Tradition and Experiment in Modern Sculpture*. American University Press, 1949.

CULTURAL AND HISTORICAL BACKGROUND

Andrews, Wayne, *Architecture, Ambition and Americans*. Harper & Bros., 1947.

Baudelaire, Charles, *Art in Paris, 1845-1862. Salons and Other Exhibitions*. Translated and edited by Jonathan Mayne. Phaidon Press, Ltd., London, 1965.

Brogan, D. W., *The Development of Modern France, 1870-1939.* * Harper Torchbooks, 1966.

Duncan, Isadora, *My Life*. Boni & Liveright, 1927.

Goncourt, Edmond and Jules de, *Pages from The Goncourt Journal*. Edited and translated by Robert Baldick. Oxford University Press, London, 1962.

Josephson, Matthew, *Victor Hugo*. Doubleday & Co., Inc., 1946.

Maurois, André:
   Olympio: The Life of Victor Hugo. Harper & Bros., 1956.
   Prometheus: The Life of Balzac. Harper and Row, 1966.

Painter, George D., *Proust: The Early Years*. Little, Brown and Co., 1963.

Quennell, Peter, *Baudelaire and the Symbolists*. Weidenfeld and Nicolson, London, 1954.

Skinner, Cornelia Otis, *Elegant Wits and Grand Horizontals*. Houghton Mifflin Co., 1962.

Symons, Arthur, *Studies in Seven Arts*. Dutton & Co., 1925.

Zola, Émile, *Salons*. Collected by F. W. Jennings and R. L. Areis. Minard, Paris, 1959.

187

Picture Credits

The sources for the illustrations in this book appear below. Credits for pictures from left to right are separated by semicolons, from top to bottom by dashes.

All the works of Auguste Rodin reproduced in this book as well as those of Edgar Degas *(page 68)*, Aristide Maillol *(pages 178-179)* and Henri Matisse and Pablo Picasso *(page 176)* are published by arrangement with SPADEM by French Reproduction Rights, Inc. The works of Jean Arp *(page 183)*, Émile-Antoine Bourdelle *(page 175)*, Constantin Brancusi *(page 182)*, Alexander Calder *(page 185)* and Alberto Giacometti *(page 180)* appear by arrangement with ADAGP by French Reproduction Rights, Inc.

SLIPCASE—Lee Boltin.

FRONT END PAPERS—Lee Boltin.

BACK END PAPERS—Lee Boltin.

CHAPTER 1: 6—Edward Steichen. 9—Collection Robert Descharnes. 11—Top original Elvira, Munich. Photographs copied by Paul Jensen courtesy The Dance Collection, Research Library of the Performing Arts, The New York Public Library at Lincoln Center. 14—Bernard Hoffman. 15—Jacques André. 18—O. E. Nelson—Lee Boltin. Both courtesy Joseph H. Hirshhorn Collection. 21 through 35—Dmitri Kessel.
CHAPTER 2: 36—J. R. Eyerman. 38—Collection Robert Descharnes except bottom Lee Boltin. 41—Collection Robert Descharnes. 42—Charles Aubry courtesy Collection Robert Descharnes—Lee Boltin. 47—Dmitri Kessel. 48—Collection Robert Descharnes; H. W. Janson. 49—H. W. Janson. 50—Frank Lerner. 53, 54, 55—Dmitri Kessel. 56—Helga Photo Studio, Inc. courtesy Bernard Black Gallery. 57—Bernard Black Gallery—O. E. Nelson courtesy Bernard Black Gallery. 58, 59—Carlo Bavagnoli. 60, 61—Dmitri Kessel. 62—Carlo Bavagnoli. 63—Dmitri Kessel.
CHAPTER 3: 64—Robert Descharnes. 66—Rudomine Studios, Paris. 68—Metropolitan Museum of Art photo—Leonard Von Matt from Rapho Guillumette. 69 —Lee Boltin—Marvin Lichtner from PIX, Inc. 70—Eddy Van der Veen from *Rodin Céramiste* by Roger Marx (1907), in the Cabinet des Estampes, Bibliothèque Nationale, Paris. 73—Culver Pictures. 75—César courtesy Collection Robert Descharnes—Fred Lyon from Rapho Guillumette. 77, 78, 79—Lee Boltin. 80 —Robert Descharnes; Lee Boltin. 81—Lee Boltin. 82—Lee Boltin except bottom right Robert Descharnes. 83—Lee Boltin except top right Pierre Boulat.
CHAPTER 4: 84—J. R. Eyerman. 86—Collection Robert Descharnes. 89—Alinari. 90—Collection Robert Descharnes. 92—Eddy Van der Veen from *Les Fleurs du Mal* by Charles Baudelaire (1940 ed.). 95, 97 through 100—Dmitri Kessel. 101—J. R. Eyerman—Lee Boltin. 102—Dmitri Kessel. 103—Scala. 104 through 107—Dmitri Kessel. 108 through 111—Lee Boltin.
CHAPTER 5: 112—Pierre Boulat. 114, 115—Lee Boltin. 117—Collection Robert Descharnes—Lee Boltin. 118—Eddy Van der Veen from *Gazette des Beaux-Arts* (1902)—H. Roger-Viollet. 121—Nadar courtesy Bulloz—Archives Photographiques. 122—Lee Boltin. 123—Eddy Van der Veen from *L'Illustre Amusant* (May 1899)—Collection Robert Descharnes. 125, 126—Lee Boltin. 127— Robert Descharnes. 128, 129—Lee Boltin. 130—Patricia Maye. 131, 132 —Paul Jensen. 133—Patricia Maye. 134, 135—Lee Boltin. 136, 137—Robert Descharnes. 138—Robert Descharnes; Lee Boltin—Lee Boltin; Robert Descharnes. 139—Lee Boltin.
CHAPTER 6: 140—Lee Boltin. 143—Collection Robert Descharnes. 144—Robert Descharnes from *Jugend* (1907). 147—H. Roger-Viollet; Lee Boltin. 151—H. Roger-Viollet—Sotheby & Co., London. 152—J. F. Limet courtesy Collection Robert Descharnes—Collection Robert Descharnes; H. Roger-Viollet. 153—Collection Robert Descharnes except top right Brown Brothers. 154—H. Roger-Viollet—Collection Robert Descharnes; Brown Brothers. 155—Collection Robert Descharnes. 157—Carlo Bavagnoli. 158 through 161—J. R. Eyerman. 162, 163—Robert Descharnes.
CHAPTER 7: 164—Lee Boltin. 168—Francis Miller courtesy The Estate of Ernest Durig. 169—Courtesy The Art Institute of Chicago—Herb Orth courtesy The Estate of Ernest Durig. 171—Pierre Choumoff courtesy Collection Robert Descharnes. 172, 173—Catherine Ireys from *Les Cathédrales de France* by Auguste Rodin (1914), in the New York Public Library. 175—Robert E. Mates courtesy Joseph H. Hirshhorn Collection. 176, 177—O. E. Nelson; Adolph Studly; Lee Boltin. All courtesy Joseph H. Hirshhorn Collection. 178, 179—Eliot Elisofon courtesy Museum of Modern Art, New York. 180—Lee Boltin courtesy Museum of Modern Art, New York. 181—©Museum of Modern Art, New York—Robert E. Mates courtesy Joseph H. Hirshhorn Collection. 182—Nina Leen. 183—A. J. Wyatt courtesy Philadelphia Museum of Art. 184—Lee Boltin courtesy Joseph H. Hirshhorn Collection. 185—©Museum of Modern Art, New York.

Acknowledgments

For their help in the preparation of this book, the author and editors wish to thank the following persons and institutions: Edith Adams, Librarian, Cooper-Hewitt Museum of Decorative Arts and Design, Smithsonian Institution, New York; Catherine Bélenger, Service des Relations Extérieures du Musée du Louvre, Paris; Annie Braunwald, Chargée de Mission au Musée du Petit Palais, Paris; Adeline Cacan, Conservateur du Musée du Petit Palais, Paris; Robert Descharnes, Paris; Mrs. Jefferson Dickson, Beverly Hills; Rhodia Dufet, Conservateur Adjoint du Musée Bourdelle, Paris; Anna Duncan, New York; André Dunoyer de Segonzac, Paris; Professor Albert E. Elsen, Stanford University, Stanford; Cécile Goldscheider, Conservateur du Musée Rodin, Paris; Ami Guichard, Lausanne; Madame Guynet-Pechadre, Conservateur, Service Photographique, Musée du Louvre, Paris; Mr. and Mrs. Joseph H. Hirshhorn, New York; Abram Lerner, Curator, and Cynthia Jaffee, Assistant Curator, Joseph H. Hirshhorn Collection, New York; Alain Lesieutre, Antiquaire, Paris; Edith Lionne, Assistante du Conservateur du Musée Rodin, Paris; Grace Mayer, Museum of Modern Art, New York; New York Public Library; Marjorie Pickens, New York; H. Roger-Viollet, Paris; Michel Sineux, Paris; John Tancock, Curator, Rodin Museum, Philadelphia; Comte Jules Tarnowski, Traveller's Club, Paris; J. Kirk T. Varnedoe, Stanford University, Stanford; Hobart Lyle Williams, Philadelphia; Anita Zahn, New York.

Index

The text for this book was photocomposed in Bodoni Book, a typeface named for its Italian designer, Giambattista Bodoni (1740-1813). One of the earliest modern typefaces, Bodoni Book differs from more evenly weighted old-style characters in the greater contrast between thick and thin parts of letters. The Bodoni character is vertical with a thin, straight serif.

x

PRODUCTION STAFF FOR TIME INCORPORATED

John L. Hallenbeck (Vice President and Director of Production),
Robert E. Foy and Caroline Ferri
Text photocomposed under the direction of Albert J. Dunn